Mountain Jews

Customs and Daily Life
in the Caucasus

Edited by
Liya Mikdash-Shamailov

The Israel Museum, Jerusalem

The Israel Museum, Jerusalem

Mountain Jews
Customs and Daily Life in the Caucasus

Fall 2001 – Fall 2002

Caroline and Joseph Gruss Gallery,
Charles Goldman Gallery,
Davide and Irene Sala Wing for Israel Communities

Curator-in-charge: Rivka Gonen
Curator of the exhibition: Liya Mikdash-Shamailov
Assistant to the curator: Edna Azriel

Exhibition design: Michal Aldor
Exhibit installation consultant: Alia Ben-Ami

Associate editors of the English catalogue:
Daisy Raccah-Djivre, Orpa Slapak
Catalogue design: Masha Pozina
Translation from the Hebrew: Edward Levin,
Etka Liebowitz, David Louvish, Gabriel Sivan
Editing: Annie Lopez, with Natalie Mendelsohn
Copy editing: Anna Barber

Photographs: Avshalom Avital, Peter Lanyi
Field photography: Liya Mikdash-Shamailov,
Boris Khaimovich, Faig Gonagov, Rivka Gonen,
Michael Kheifets, Gamlet Gasanov, Mikhail Kirilov

Color separations and plates: Graphor Ltd., Tel Aviv
Printing: Kal Press Ltd., Tel Aviv

Catalogue no. 474
ISBN 965 278 315 3

The exhibition and catalogue were made possible by

The Israeli Ministry of Absorption

JDC Israel

The Forchheimer Fund for Ethnographic
Exhibitions, New York

The Aaron Beare Foundation, Durban

Bruce Kovner, New York

Dan and Cary Bronner, Düsseldorf

The donors to the Israel Museum's 2001
Exhibition Fund: Ruth and Leon Davidoff,
Paris and Mexico City; Hanno D. Mott, New York;
The Nash Family Foundation, New York

The donors to the Museum's Share 2000 Program

Illustration on pp. 15, 49, and 121:
Detail of the facade of a house in Vartashen
Photo: Boris Khaimovich

On the cover:
Woman rinsing vessels in boiling water for Passover,
Kuba, Azerbaijan, 1996
Photo: Liya Mikdash-Shamailov

Contents

All the measurements are given in centimeters.
H = height, W = width, L = length, D = diameter

Greetings

I came to know and appreciate the community known as "Mountain Jews" during my term of office as Minister of Absorption in 1992–96. This community, whose roots in the Caucasus date back to more than 1,500 years ago, preserved its Jewish identity and developed a culture of its own in a region populated by a host of different peoples and plagued by ethnic tensions.

Sincere thanks are due to all those who helped organize this exhibition, first and foremost Liya Mikdash-Shamailov. It gives me great pleasure to have had the opportunity to lend a hand in this important endeavor.

It is my hope that the exhibition will attract large crowds, enabling as broad a public as possible to get a glimpse of this distant but fascinating culture. Promoting a better understanding of this community will undoubtedly help in the assimilation of its members into Israeli society.

Yair Tsaban
Former Minister of Absorption

I would like to extend warm congratulations to the people who initiated this exhibition about the Mountain Jews and to all those who helped organize it.

While many people do not distinguish between Caucasian Jews and immigrants from the former Soviet Union in general, I believe that the community of Mountain Jews deserves special attention in view of its distinctive character and culture.

The Caucasian community is remarkable for its love of the land of Israel and for the way it managed to preserve its Jewish heritage over the ages in spite of its geographical isolation. These aspects, clearly conveyed in the exhibition and catalogue, make this project an important contribution to Israeli culture.

On the occasion of the opening of the exhibition, I offer the members of the Caucasian community my most sincere hopes that they will remain the warm and close-knit community that we have learnt to know, and will continue to contribute to the cultural melting pot of Israeli society and assimilate successfully into it.

Yuli Edelstein
Deputy Minister of Absorption

Foreword

Mountain Jews: Customs and Daily Life in the Caucasus is the tenth in a series of exhibitions organized by the Museum's Department of Jewish Ethnography about the communities of the Jewish world, both in Israel and in the Diaspora.

Caucasian Jews began to immigrate to Palestine as early as the mid-nineteenth century. The Caucasian community has nonetheless remained one of the least known in Israeli society, and it is only the major waves of immigration of the 1970s and 1990s, which raised its numbers in Israel to approximately 80,000, that have helped to bring a long-overdue focus to the community. We therefore present this exhibition with a twofold objective: to enlighten our public about a rich and heretofore little-known dimension of world Jewish cultural heritage; and to assist in the integration of the members of this unique community into Israeli society.

While the Mountain Jews were scattered among Muslim peoples over a vast area of the Caucasus, they remained deeply committed to their Jewish identity, and their culture evolved into a distinctive blend of Jewish and local customs and traditions. The exhibition and its accompanying publication present highlights of the material and spiritual aspects of this culture, offering our public a glimpse into a world that is both very familiar and, to many among us, still very remote.

Preparing an exhibition and book about such a far-flung community, involving research under sometimes perilous conditions, has been no simple feat. We are deeply grateful to all of those whose generous support enabled us to embark on this project and to realize it fully, including: the donors to the Museum's 2001 Exhibition Fund – Ruth and Leon Davidoff, Paris and Mexico City; Hanno D. Mott, New York; and The Nash Family Foundation, New York – and to its Share 2000 Program; the Ministry of Absorption; JDC Israel; the Forchheimer Fund for Ethnographic Exhibitions, New York; the Aaron Beare Foundation, Durban; Bruce Kovner, New York; and Dan and Cary Bronner, Düsseldorf.

Finally, our greatest debt of gratitude goes to Liya Mikdash-Shamailov, curator of the exhibition, who pursued her assignment with undaunted spirit despite daunting obstacles; and to Dr. Rivka Gonen, Senior Curator of Jewish Ethnography and the motivating force for this enterprise, for whom this project crowns a long and distinguished career in the Museum. Together with the Museum's dedicated staff, they brought to fruition a project of singular complexity and significance.

James S. Snyder
Anne and Jerome Fisher Director

Population Centers of the Mountain Jews

Map legend:
- ■ Capital city
- ● City with a Jewish population
- District border
- State boundary

0   100   200 km

Preface

Situated between the Black and the Caspian Sea, the Caucasian mountain range stretches over more than 1,000 kilometers and forms a geographical barrier between the Russian steppes and the northern parts of the Middle East. The mountains are so high and rugged that apart from one narrow pass at the heart of the range, the only way to cross them is through the roads that border the Caspian and the Black Sea. As a result of this mountainous topography, the peoples of the Caucasus are divided into a myriad of small ethnic entities, each endowed with its own language and often unable to communicate with its closest neighbors. The region, which attracted peoples and tribes from the earliest of times because of the protection that its harsh features afford, boasts one of the largest numbers of ethnic groups and languages in the world. Over the centuries, neighboring powers such as Persia, the Ottoman Empire, and Russia repeatedly attempted to conquer it, but they were always met with Caucasian revolts. These revolts, together with the frequent internal strifes that tore apart the peoples of the Caucasus, have led the region to be perceived as dangerous and politically unstable.

The Caucasus was part of the Soviet Union until its dissolution in the 1990s. Today, the regions that lie to the north of the Caucasian mountain range consist of autonomous Muslim entities within Russia, while the areas to the south are divided into three independent countries: Georgia and Armenia, which are ancient Christian states, and Azerbaijan, a Muslim state that was established in 1920 by the Soviet government, unifying a host of small provinces and principalities that were formerly ruled by various foreign powers.

The Jews of the Caucasus comprise two distinct communities: the Jews of Georgia, who live in a Christian environment, and the Mountain Jews, who are scattered across a vast area in the east and north of the Caucasus – mainly northern Azerbaijan and Dagestan – and live among Muslim peoples. According to their own traditions, both groups reached the Caucasus in the first millennium BCE. While both remained deeply committed to their Jewish heritage in spite of recurring waves of oppression, each eventually absorbed some of the local customs and traditions of the surrounding peoples, evolving into two distinct communities. This exhibition and its accompanying catalogue focus on the Mountain Jews, and the term "Caucasian Jews" should henceforth be understood to refer solely to this community, and not to the Jews of Georgia.

The idea of organizing an exhibition about the Mountain Jews was initially raised by the Absorption Ministry under Yair Tsaban in 1995. When I was first approached on this matter, I knew almost nothing about this community, and was fortunate to be put in contact with Liya Mikdash-Shamailov, curator of the exhibition and herself a member of the Caucasian community. Liya devoted herself wholeheartedly to the project, putting to excellent use her knowledge of the various languages and customs of the community, visiting the settlements of Caucasian Jews throughout the country, and traveling a number of times to the Caucasus to gather information and objects.

In preparing this exhibition and catalogue, the fruit of many years of field work and extensive research, we benefited from the assistance and support of many institutions, community leaders, and prominent scholars. We extend our heartfelt thanks to the Lavon Institute, Tel Aviv; the Ben-Zvi Institute, Jerusalem; the Central Zionist Archives, Jerusalem; the Central Archives for the History of the Jewish People, The Hebrew University of Jerusalem; Beth Hatefutsoth, The Nahum Goldmann Museum of the Jewish Diaspora, Tel Aviv; the Haifa Museum of Ethnology; the Archives of the Jerusalem Municipality and the Archives of the Tel Aviv Municipality, who gave us access to documents and photographs; and the collectors Bill Gross, Tel Aviv, and Eliezer Mizrahi, Carmiel, who graciously loaned us objects for the exhibition. Without the generosity and dedication of all those mentioned above, this project could not have been realized.

Dr. Rivka Gonen
Senior Curator of Jewish Ethnography

From the Caucasus to Jerusalem

Despite the Soviet regime's attempts to make them an integral part of the Russian people, Caucasian Jews have preserved their Jewish national identity. Since they maintain *shehitah* (kosher slaughter), circumcise their newborn sons, and marry within the community, assimilation poses no threat to their traditional heritage. Anyone seeking the origin of their nickname, "Mountain Jews," must go back to Russia's occupation of the Caucasus in the early nineteenth century. After that campaign the Czar sent a representative to the Caucasus whose task it was to prepare a report on the ethnic groups inhabiting the region. In his report the official made reference to Jews living in the mountains (for fear of pogroms) who seemed unlike Russian Jews in their outward appearance, mode of life, dress, and vernacular. To distinguish them from their Russian brethren, he coined the term "Mountain Jews."

Problems arising from the integration of the Mountain Jews in Israel led members of the staff of the Absorption Ministry who initiated this exhibition to choose to portray the Mountain Jews from the angle of their settlement in Israel immediately after arriving here, stressing their share in Israel's upbuilding rather than focusing on traditional ethnographic matters — without, of course, underrating the part played by their life in the Caucasus, their yearning for the old homeland, and their ties with that region.

As a Jew of Caucasian origin, I was happy to accept the invitation to mount this exhibition, as I felt that it would enable me to blend a scientific interest in the community with my own special affinity with its culture. I also believed that organizing it would present no difficulty, since I speak fluent Tat, Azerbaijani, and Russian, the major languages of the Caucasus region, and have close family living there. In the collection of field study material I did indeed receive much help from my mother, Esther, and my late father, Aharon. Specialized knowledge and personal contacts should have made my task an easy one, yet things turned out to be more complex than I had anticipated.

Most of the field work was conducted in Azerbaijan, owing to restrictions imposed by the security situation in other areas. I did obtain a special permit to enter Dagestan, but it was limited to a stay of three days only, which meant that I did not have time to gather sufficient material there. Some of the items displayed in the exhibition were purchased by me in the course of two journeys to the Caucasus and others were received as gifts. Organizing this exhibition also involved meeting with numerous Caucasian families who had immigrated to Israel from Azerbaijan, Dagestan, Kabardino-Balkaria, Chechnya, and Stavropol. Rumors of the forthcoming exhibition took flight and many members of the community lent or even donated objects to the Museum; unfortunately, numerous families that I met had left such items behind, never imagining that they were of any value.

I have done my utmost to convey the cultural diversity of the Mountain Jews, but should anyone feel that I have not done justice to them, I hope they will forgive me. I also offer an apology to all who contacted me with suggestions as to how this exhibition — which in my view is geared to the general public but especially to Jews of Caucasian origin — might best be presented. I have endeavored to respond to the various requests, knowing that I could not hope to please everyone. As a member of the Caucasian Jewish community, I too have felt great surges of emotion at different stages in the course of this project, but I have tried to remain faithful to the rules of objectivity dictated by the Museum.

A great number of individuals and institutions have helped me to realize this exhibition and catalogue, and I remain deeply endebted to them. Special thanks are due to Yair Tsaban, the former Minister of Absorption, and to Edna Bustin and Dr. David Ben-Yosef, members of his staff. I am likewise grateful to Yuli Edelstein, Deputy Minister (and former Minister) of Absorption, to Boris Maftsir, former Director General of that ministry, and to Ya'akov Bar-Shimon, another member of its staff.

I also wish to thank Ilman Elipolatov, Deputy Director of Dagestan Television, Kamil Mamidov, head of Azerbaijan Television's Public Relations Department, and Dr. Emil Kirimov of the Baku Academy of Sciences, for their valuable assistance.

Without the substantial help of the Jewish communities in Dagestan and Azerbaijan and without the interest that they displayed, I would not have been able to mount this exhibition. My warmest thanks are therefore extended to members of the Kuba community and to those officiating in its synagogue, as well as to Boris Simanduyev, the community's leader, and Natan Eliaguyev; to members of the Baku community and their leader, Simon Ikhyilov; to members of the Oguz community and their leader, Boris Shamailov; to the Kabardino-Balkaria community; to Svetlana Danielova; and to Shimi Didayev and David Davidov, members of the Makhachkala and Derbent communities respectively. I am especially grateful to the Israel Embassy staff in Azerbaijan, to former Ambassador Arkadi Milman, and to Peter Shofet, Israel's former Consul in Baku.

I wish to express my heartfelt thanks to the staff members of the Makhachkala and Derbent museums; to those of the Azerbaijan Historical Museum in Baku; and to the three photographers who worked with me: Faig Gonagov (Kuba), Gamlet Gasanov (Baku), and Mikhail Kirilov (Makhachkala).

In Israel I had the assistance of Prof. Michael Zand and Prof. Mordechai Altshuler of The Hebrew University of Jerusalem, who also contributed articles to this catalogue, for which I am deeply grateful. Special thanks are due to Prof. Daniel Sperber, who was kind enough to read some of the chapters and to give this work the benefit of his expertise in the customs of various Jewish communities; and to Dr. Dan Shapira of the Open University, who transliterated into English the Judeo-Tat terms in the catalogue with dedication and expertise. I would also like to extend warm thanks to Esther Juhasz and Dalit Thon, for helping me to select items from the Haifa Museum collection, and to the anthropologist Chen Bram.

I am greatly beholden to many members of the Israel Museum staff. Dr. Rivka Gonen, Senior Curator of Jewish Ethnography and curator-in-charge of this exhibition, offered help and support through every stage of the project; without her assistance, it might never have been completed. Dr. Iris Fishof, Director of Curatorial Services, helped coordinate the project and supervised its progress. Special thanks are due to Daisy Raccah-Djivre, Chief Curator of the Judaica and Jewish Ethnography Department, who appreciated the difficulties I faced while organizing the exhibition and helped me surmount them; Orpa Slapak, who read the entire Hebrew catalogue, offering many insightful comments, and helped in ever possible way; and Ester Muchawsky-Schnapper, who graciously agreed to read the entire English manuscript before it went to press. Edna Azriel worked faithfully on the exhibition and catalogue, extending support and advice at every stage, and all my colleagues in the department were at my disposal whenever guidance was required: Alia Ben-Ami, Rachel Sarfati, Lucci Lang, Chaya Benjamin, Tchiya Sapir, Chen Mellul, No'am Bar'am-Ben Yossef, Ora Shwartz-Be'eri, Sara Gal, and the late Natalia Polyatchek. Thanks are also due to our dedicated volunteers, Miryam Adler and Shmuel Korn.

I would also like to express my warm appreciation to Michael Maggen, Marina Rassovsky, Kochavit Shiryon, Ludmila Hodorkovsky, and Michael Barcik of the Museum's Conservation and Restoration Laboratories; to Dor Lin, head of the Marketing and Public Relations Department; to Nirit Zur, head of the Publications Department, and her staff – especially Tirtsa Barri, who designed the Hebrew version of the catalogue with taste and sensitivity, and Revital Mazover, who edited it, contributing much to its style and content; Masha Pozina, who brought her considerable talent to the design of the English version, and Annie Lopez, who edited it with great care and devotion; and Yael Golan, who offered skillful technical support at various stages of the work. I am also grateful to members of the Exhibition Design Department, headed by Halina Hamou – notably Michal Aldor, the exhibition's designer, who managed to conjure a far-off world within the narrow confines of a museum gallery; and to Pesach Ruder, Alex Markov, Moris Lasry, Menachem Amin, Artur Avakov, and Dan Divinsky of the Department's technical staff, who helped her do so.

As a veteran Caucasian immigrant and the mother of children raised and educated in Israel, I am glad to have had the opportunity of linking the two worlds that fashioned my own identity. It is my hope that the exhibition will serve to bring those two worlds closer together.

Liya Mikdash-Shamailov
Curator of the Exhibition

Note to the reader:
Judeo-Tat, the language of the Mountain Jews, comprises a
multiplicity of different dialects. The transliteration of Tat terms
into English in this book reflects the dialect spoken by its
editor, Liya Mikdash-Shamailov, who is from Kuba, Azerbaijan.
The transcription follows pronunciation rather than phonetic
rules, as closely as possible
x - sounds like the Hebrew h
ḥ - sounds like the Arabic h (a slightly softer version of x)
gh is a guttural sound
q is a softer version of gh
ü - sounds like the French u

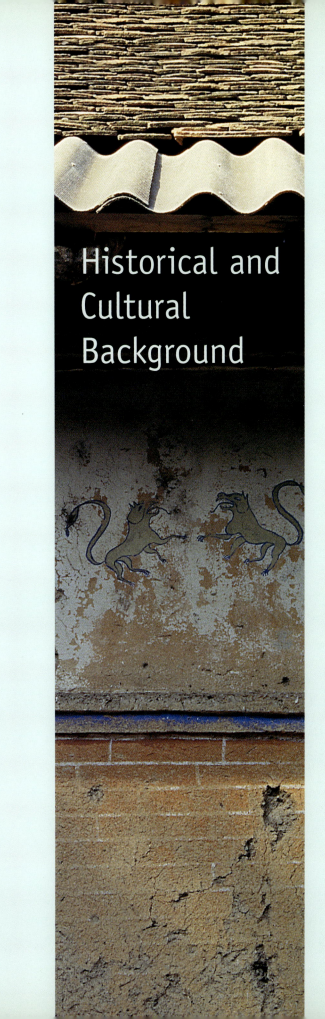

Historical and Cultural Background

A History of the Mountain Jews
Mordechai Altshuler

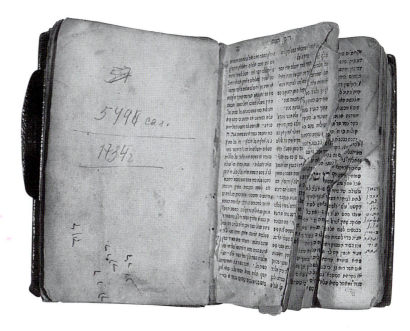

The Mountain Jews, or *Juhur* as they called themselves, belong to one of the oldest communities in the Jewish people. According to a tradition once prevalent among the members of the community, they are descended from the ten tribes that were exiled from the Kingdom of Israel in the eighth century BCE. While this tradition is obscure and cannot be verified, there were certainly Jewish communities in the eastern Caucasus as early as the third century CE. Many Jews escaped persecution in Persia by fleeing to the Caucasus just across the borders of the Persian Empire, bringing their language – Judeo-Tat, which belongs to the group of Iranian languages – with them. The name of a scholar of the community mentioned in the Jerusalem Talmud – Rabbi Simeon Safra of "Terbent" – probably reveals a connection with the city of Derbent. The Jews settled in the mountainous regions of the eastern Caucasus, building their villages in the narrow gorges between the mountains and near water sources. Thanks to their isolation, they were able to preserve the unique customs and language that they had brought with them from Persia. At this early stage, therefore, the Mountain Jews belonged to the cultural sphere of Persian Jewry.

During the seventh and eighth centuries the eastern Caucasus, where the Mountain Jews were living, was shaken by a series of wars between the Khazars from the north and the Arabs. The Khazar kingdom practiced religious tolerance, and the ruling elite even adopted the Jewish religion. In regions overrun by the Arabs, however, thousands of Jews were forcibly converted to Islam, though they continued to use Judeo-Tat and to maintain some Jewish customs. Such attempts at forcible conversion frequently aroused resistance. Many Jews preferred to die as martyrs rather than become Muslims, while others took part in armed uprisings against the Arab rulers of the region. Not surprisingly, many of them found refuge from the cruelty of the Arab rulers in the Khazar kingdom, and the Jewish population of the kingdom increased considerably.

The centuries of Khazar-Arab warfare weakened the links between the Mountain Jews in the eastern Caucasus and the Jewish community of Iran, and a spiritual center of scholars, doctors, and astrologers took shape among the Mountain Jews. This center was already in existence at the time of the Mongol invasion in the thirteenth century. By then, some of the local Muslim rulers had adopted different attitudes; policies of forcible conversion to Islam, which had driven out many Jews, were replaced by a willingness to protect the Jews, whom they now considered an important source of income.

"The Cut Book" –
three books bound
together: *Or Na'arav* (?);
*Commentary on the Day of
Atonement Prayers* (Venice,
1587); and *Tuv ha-Aretz*
(Venice, 1655)[1]
Paper, leather binding
Lent by Abraham Frohlich,
Jerusalem

Opposite:
Jewish cemetery, in use
from the early 18th
century to the late 19th
century, Karchagi,
Dagestan, 1999

A representative of the committee of the Kuba community (Krasnaya Sloboda), appointed by the Soviet authorities, receives members of the community, 1920s
Photo courtesy of Haim Agarunov, Hadera

During the fourteenth century the region suffered from violent incursions by Mongol tribes; in the fifteenth century, the Ottoman Empire and the Persian kingdom fought fiercely for control of the area. As a consequence, many Jewish residents of the coastal areas and the foothills fled to small, isolated mountain villages, seeking refuge from the robbery and murder that unavoidably accompanied the wars. Between the fourteenth and sixteenth centuries, the Mountain Jews experienced a spiritual decline. Nevertheless, despite being cut off from the Jewish centers outside the Caucasus and despite the lack of local scholars, the Jews in the mountain villages continued to maintain their ancestral traditions as well as they could; these traditions frequently contained traces of customs and beliefs taken over from the local peoples (see the chapter on beliefs and ceremonies, pp. 111–19).

The eighteenth century again saw the Caucasus as an arena of clashes and competition between the three neighboring powers – Persia, the Ottoman Empire, and Russia. As a result, local princes, supported alternately by one of these powers, gained ascendancy. They taxed the Jews at a higher rate than the rest of the population, also forcing them to engage in degrading professions and enlisting them in their armies. Centuries of warfare taught the Jews to protect themselves and their property, and they became one of the few Jewish communities whose members were familiar with weapons and were accomplished horseback riders. These skills, however, could not save them from the punitive expeditions led by the Persian ruler Nadir Shah in the 1730s. These expeditions left many communities in ruins; many Jews were cruelly slaughtered and others were compelled to adopt Islam. There were considerable numbers of crypto-Jews, that is, Jews who openly adopted Islam but maintained their Judaism in their homes. The unrestrained cruelty of some rulers could be avoided and the existence of the community ensured by seeking the protection of a strong local ruler. One of the strongest principalities in the region in the last quarter of the eighteenth century was that of Kuba, under Fath-Ali-Khan. This ruler granted the Jews privileges in which their rights and duties were defined; he allowed the Jews to return to Derbent and permitted Jews from the neighboring villages to settle in the principality's capital city (also named Kuba). It was only natural that Jews from many local villages flocked to the principality of Kuba, mainly to its capital city, which in time earned the nickname of "Jerusalem of the Caucasus."

At the beginning of the nineteenth century, the Jews of the eastern Caucasus welcomed the advent of Russian rule, as they believed that Russia would be able to bring about the long-awaited pacification of the region. The Russians did not discriminate against the Jews, who enjoyed freedom of religion and of occupation among other local peoples and were allowed to settle wherever they wished. Links were thus forged between the Mountain Jews and the Jews of Russia. The Mountain Jews gave the small number of Jews serving in the Russian army a hearty welcome, and hospitably received the few Jews who settled among them. As years passed, young Mountain Jews went to study at Lithuanian yeshivot, some of them ultimately returning to their communities to serve as rabbis and leaders. In time, East-European Jewry exerted increasing influence over the Mountain Jews, and the new scholarly elite made strenuous efforts to purge the community's customs of traces left by centuries of non-Jewish influence. One of the most prominent communal leaders was Rabbi Ya'akov Yitzhaki, who established a yeshivah at Derbent to educate a younger generation of ritual slaughterers and rabbis. Thanks to the untiring efforts of rabbis in Derbent and Kuba, synagogue congregations gradually increased. Some members of the community began to attend Russian schools. At the close of the century, the first university student from among the Mountain Jews, Ilya Sharbatovich Anisimov, returned from Moscow, to become the first ethnographer of his community. His father, Sharbat, son of Nissim Anisimov, immigrated to Jerusalem and was one of the founders of the Mountain Jews' community in the Holy City.

The hope of redemption was an integral part of the traditions and customs of Mountain Jews. Such nebulous longings became more palpable when *shaddarim* (rabbinical emissaries) began to reach the region to collect funds for the Jewish communities in the land of Israel – Jerusalem, Hebron, Tiberias, and Safed. By the mid-nineteenth century, the number of wealthy Jews had increased. They received the emissaries with open arms and gave them generous contributions. Towards the end of the century, growing numbers of Mountain Jews were immigrating to the Holy Land. Some settled there permanently, while others returned to the Caucasus, bringing with them descriptions of life in the land of Israel. The emissaries and the immigrants became living links between the community of Mountain Jews and the land of Israel.

The early years of the twentieth century saw increasing Zionist influence, both political and cultural, on the Mountain Jews. Zionism provided a bridge between the community and European Jewry, resulting in cooperation that ultimately produced the first prayer book with a Judeo-Tat translation, published in 1909. After World War I, the first newspaper in Judeo-Tat, *Mountain Echo*, appeared; it betrayed strong Zionist leanings. Under the influence of the new Zionist ideas, changes occurred in the Mountain Jews' educational system, and schools established during the first decades of the twentieth century gave considerable attention to the study of Hebrew and Hebrew grammar, Jewish history and land-of-Israel studies. Mountain Jews began to immigrate to Palestine not merely to pray at the ancestral graves but to take part in the rebuilding of the new Jewish commonwealth in the Holy Land.

The new ideas being espoused in certain circles of Russian Jewry were soon taken up by young Mountain Jews. Like their East-European brethren, they were eager to combine social justice with the

Mountain Jews in the army of the Czar, Russia, 1896
Photo courtesy of Beth Hatefutsoth, The Nahum Goldmann Museum of the Jewish Diaspora, Tel Aviv

Members of a Jewish
kolhoz celebrate the 15th
anniversary of the
Kabardino-Balkaria
Republic, Nalchik, 1933
Photo courtesy of Svetlana
Danilova, Nalchik

establishment of a national home for the Jews in the land of Israel. One of these young men was Yehezkel, son of Shimon Nisanov, who immigrated to Palestine in 1906. Having witnessed the massacre of many Armenians by Azerbaijanis in 1905, he understood the importance of establishing a Jewish self-defense force that would be able to protect the Jews and their possessions.

During World War I, the Russian Revolution, and the Civil War (1914–21), the Mountain Jews suffered from attacks by their Muslim neighbors. Many Jewish villages were destroyed and rural Jews had to abandon their homes and settle in towns and cities. Like Russian Jewry in general, the Mountain Jews became part of the national and Zionist revival of those days, and young members of the community were ready to immigrate in large numbers to take part in the defense and rebuilding of the national home. In a letter written in 1919, Chaim Weizmann, later Israel's first president, referred to "thousands of young Jews who had served in the Russian army, Mountain Jews from the Caucasus . . . healthy, well-trained young men . . . begging to immigrate to the land of Israel to participate in its building." Only a few, however, were able to achieve their goal and reach the land of Israel, after considerable trials and tribulations. When the Soviet authorities consolidated their control of the eastern Caucasus in the early 1920s, they made efforts to spread their ideology among the Mountain Jews as well. Soviet schools were established for the community's children, in which the

language was Judeo-Tat, written in the Hebrew alphabet. The new government also encouraged the development of Judeo-Tat literature, which had begun to flourish many years before, and promoted the formation of theater troupes performing in Judeo-Tat. In order to help the community extricate itself from the economic crisis of the Civil War years, Jewish residents were granted plots of land and Jewish villages were built. Unlike the situation with regard to Russian Jewry as a whole, Soviet activities did not normally clash with Jewish tradition, and the Mountain Jews were allowed to maintain their national identity.

At the end of the 1920s and in the early 1930s, however, the authorities adopted a new policy. Attacks on Jewish religion and tradition were stepped up, orchestrated in some cases by members of the community itself; the Hebrew alphabet was banned and replaced first by the Latin and then by the Cyrillic alphabet, among other things to cut the community's ties with its traditional and cultural roots. During the 1930s, the Soviet government promoted the view that the Mountain Jews were not part of the Jewish people at all but members of an Iranian nation (the Tats) who had settled in the region. This trend was emphasized after World War II, when the authorities conducted an expressly anti-Semitic and anti-Zionist policy. However, the attempt to sever the connection between the Mountain Jews and the Jewish people was unsuccessful, and only a few among the community lent it support.

Delegation of the Azerbaijan Republic to the 18th convention of the Communist Party, with Stalin sitting in the center. Standing in the upper row (second from right) is Ya'akov Agarunov, who served as secretary of the Oil Committee in Baku, Moscow, 1939
Photo courtesy of Mikhail Agarunov, Baku

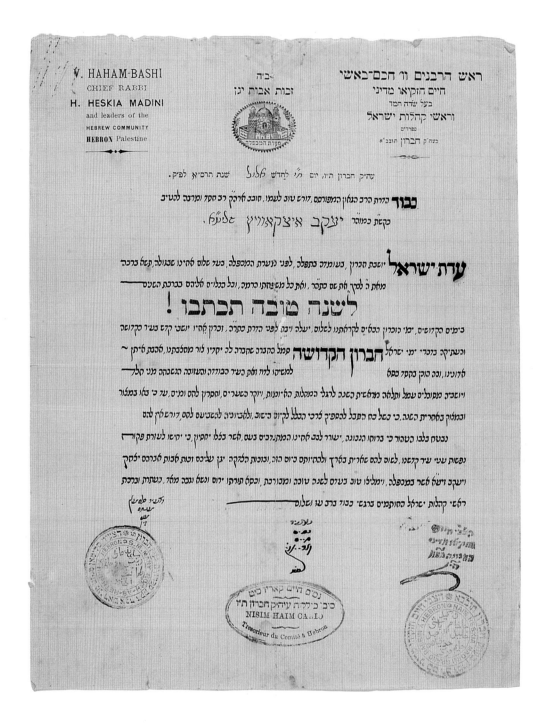

Letter from Naftali, son of Rabbi Ya'akov Yitzhaki, to Menahem Ussishkin, in which he discusses the collecting of money to purchase lands in Palestine, Derbent, Dagestan, 1902 (?)

Lent by the Central Zionist Archives, Jerusalem

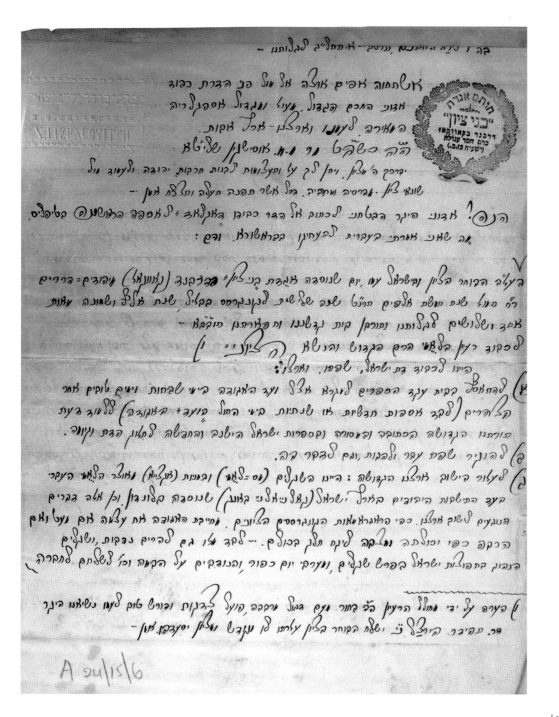

Letter from the Chief
Sephardic Rabbi in
Palestine, Haim Hizkiyahu
Medini, to Rabbi Ya'akov
Yitzhaki of Derbent, asking
for contributions to the
Jewish community of
Hebron, Hebron, 1901

Jewish woman selling her
household goods before
immigrating to Israel,
Derbent, Dagestan, 1994

The strength of the extended family, as well as traditions passed down from one generation to the next, maintained the historical continuity of the community, which persisted in seeing itself as an integral part of the Jewish people. It was only natural that the Mountain Jews upheld their national feelings, which were moreover reinforced by the establishment of the State of Israel and later by the Six-Day War. Around the time of Israel's declaration of independence, Jews gathered in synagogues to celebrate, and after the great victory of the Six-Day War many Mountain Jews joined the struggle for the right to emigrate. Their efforts bore fruit in the early 1970s, when many of them arrived in Israel. They also had a part in the mass immigration of the early 1990s. By now, most of the community resides in Israel, and its members are striving to integrate themselves among the population at large and to make their own unique contribution to the Israeli multi-culture in the making.

1   A later addition written by hand on the book recounts the "Miraculous Saving in Kuba" (1734), about an officer in the army of Nadir Shah who tried to behead a sage reading a book, but whose sword only succeeded in cutting the book (hence its title). As a result of this miracle, the officer decided to stop killing Jews. Thus, not only the sage but the entire community of Mountain Jews was saved.

Mountain Jews loading their cargo on a truck on the way to Israel, Dagestan, 1978
Photo courtesy of Beth Hatefutsoth, The Nahum Goldmann Museum of the Jewish Diaspora, Tel Aviv

Yearning for Zion:
The Immigration to Israel

Moshe Yosifov

The Jews of the Caucasus believe they are the descendants of the ten tribes exiled by the Assyrian King Shalmaneser V from the land of Israel. This tradition, coupled with their religious faith, led many Caucasian Jews to realize Zionist ideals even before the Zionist movement was established.

The Beginnings of Caucasian Immigration

We have very little information about the immigration of Caucasian Jews before the first half of the nineteenth century. Most of the Caucasian immigrants settled in the Old City of Jerusalem and endured severe economic conditions. In 1865, the community numbered about sixty people. In 1875, the local *HaLevanon* newspaper reported the following: "The Jewish immigrants from the Caucasus usually settle in Jerusalem. They number about 100 families, and have come with their own money, which they brought with them. They are peddlers, heads of families, and store owners, and they have built their own quarter and synagogue. Because they are a humble community, they haven't made their mark on Jerusalem." By 1881, 300 Jews from the city of Kuba and 200 from Dagestan lived in Jerusalem. The story of their aliyah,* the many hardships they endured on their journey, and the trials and tribulations they experienced in settling in Israel are little known, perhaps due to their natural modesty. The money for the construction of the community's synagogue in Jerusalem was donated by a prosperous man named Avraham Dadashov. The synagogue became a social and cultural meeting place for members of the community, where they could speak their own language (*Juhuri*), look for relatives, arrange marriages, provide for employment, and so forth. When the Old City of Jerusalem was conquered by the Jordanians in 1948, the Caucasian synagogue was destroyed by the Jordanian Legion.

In 1865, Rabbi Sharbat Anisimov immigrated to Jerusalem. He was a wealthy man, and he purchased land near the Lions Gate of the Old City of Jerusalem in order to build a neighborhood, yeshivah, and Talmud Torah (religious school) for Caucasian Jews. He also organized fund-raising for the poorer members of the community. Rabbi Anisimov's building plan was not implemented, and he returned to the Caucasus. In 1894, he immigrated again to Jerusalem and returned to communal activity, directing members of his community who had worked in agriculture in the Caucasus to agricultural settlement. In the same year he established the Committee of the Community of Mountain Jews (the Dagestan community) and sent letters to Baron de Hirsch and the Rothschild family in the committee's name, requesting money for the purchase of land and farm tools in order to prepare his community for agricultural work. In the Hebrew month of Shevat (January/February) 1894, he also appealed to other philanthropists through the *Havatzelet* newspaper, writing: "Please support the immigration of members of our community to Palestine . . . they desire to be colonists." Rabbi Anisimov even leased a plot of land in Jericho with his own money, hoping that his brethren would settle there and work in agriculture, thus freeing themselves from welfare support and becoming self-sufficient. The aid did not arrive and the settlement plan was never implemented.

* "Aliyah" means "ascent" in Hebrew and is used to refer to the immigration of Jews to Israel.

Opposite:
Mountain Jews participating in a Purim parade, Tel Aviv, 1934
Photo courtesy of Rivka Avshalomov, Tel Aviv

Caucasian Jews and the Zionist Movement

The establishment of the Zionist movement awakened great excitement among Caucasian Jews. After the Second Zionist Congress in 1898, a Zionist Association was founded in Baku, followed in the ensuing years by others in various locations throughout the Caucasus.

The associations dealt mainly with the dissemination of information. In 1900, they raised money in order to send Matityahu Bogatirov and Shlomo Mordechaiov – leaders of the Zionist movement in the Caucasus – as representatives to the Fourth Zionist Congress. With their sturdy build, splendid costumes, and swords hanging at their sides, they made a striking impression on the other participants. Herzl was astonished that members of the community worked in agriculture, and he predicted that they would be pioneers of agricultural work in the land of Israel. A number of Caucasian Jews were even photographed with him. These Zionist activities gave rise to the establishment of several

Mountain Jews pose with a photograph of Theodor Herzl flanked by the community's Zionist delegates to mourn his passing, Derbent, Dagestan, 1904
Photo courtesy of Lydia Tarlashinsky, Jerusalem

aliyah groups, yet in spite of this, most Caucasian Jews did not succeed in immigrating to Palestine because of a lack of funds and because they did not receive aid from Zionist organizations. On April 5, 1904, Bogatirov and Mordechaiov appealed to Herzl, requesting that he allot land for agricultural settlement to a group of thirty to forty families who wished to immigrate to Palestine immediately. There was no response to their request. In the same year, several families who had set out for Palestine remained stranded in Turkey due to a lack of funds. In 1905, a group of wealthy Caucasian Jews examined the possibility of purchasing land in Palestine. They even considered acquiring land in Transjordan, among the Muslim population, arguing that in the Caucasus too they had lived among Muslims and managed to protect themselves. However, the project was not realized. Two other groups, one comprising 600 people and the other 300, were organized in 1905–6, but they, too, could not fulfill their dream because of a lack of support.

Aliyah from the Caucasus took an unprecedented turn in 1907, when 998 Caucasian Jews immigrated to Palestine. Most of the immigrants settled in Jerusalem, about one-third in Jaffa, and approximately 100 in various settlements. In the same year the chief rabbi of Dagestan, Rabbi Ya'akov Yitzhaki, immigrated to Palestine, together with several families, and was able to realize the dream of establishing a settlement for Caucasian Jews. The group purchased 250 acres of land with their own money in a hostile region near Rishon LeZion. They moved onto the site on the third day of the festival of Hanukkah – at first only eight families, then more – and named the settlement Be'er Ya'akov, in honor of Rabbi Ya'akov Yitzhaki. Lacking any budget, the settlers built houses similar to those in which they had lived in the villages of the Caucasus – a type of sun-dried mud and stone dwelling – and planted almond trees and later other fruit trees. Water was brought from far away in small quantities. By 1910, the settlement numbered 308 inhabitants.

During World War I, the Turkish government drafted the settlement's men into forced labor at the Dead Sea. At the end of the war, a small number returned to the village and discovered that it had been destroyed and plundered. In addition to this calamity, Palestine was infested with locusts, and the settlers had to start all over again. After the war, Be'er Ya'akov was revived, and the Jewish institutions dealing with agricultural settlement asked the villagers to take in new immigrants of European origin and teach them agriculture. This was viewed as a challenge and honor by the Caucasian settlers, and they accepted and trained many new settlers.

Despite continuous efforts to procure aid from Zionist institutions in order to acquire land, no assistance came. At the initiation of Sasson Machtiev, the Jerusalem group headed by him participated in the building of the Beit Israel quarter in Jerusalem. Machtiev constructed a large building containing apartments, stores, and workshops for his community. He set up a large cowshed with a herd of premium dairy cows, as well as several hundred goats and sheep, which supplied milk and cheese products to the population of Jerusalem. The shepherds were members of the Caucasian community. Immigrants from the Caucasus were also among the first to build the Givat Shaul neighborhood in West Jerusalem in 1907. A synagogue for the Caucasian community in the Beit Israel quarter was completed in 1908 with money donated by the philanthropist Pessah Elkanah Subaiev. Shmuel Shmuelov erected a synagogue and yeshivah in the Milner quarter, near Mea She'arim, and dedicated it to immigrants from the city of Vartashen. Today, the site is abandoned and in a state of neglect.

Another attempt to establish a Caucasian settlement was undertaken in 1909. Ten families with many children, who had previously been farmers in the village of Khasavyurt in Dagestan, moved to the settlement of Mahanaim, located near the Hula Swamp. The settlement had been founded by Jews from Galicia and subsequently abandoned due to sickness, economic hardship, and the fear of Beduin attacks. Two years later, because of the same difficulties, the Caucasian settlers were also forced to abandon Mahanaim.

A well-known episode in the history of Caucasian settlement in Palestine is related to the exploits of the Ha-Shomer (watchman) organization, the first militia in Palestine. In 1908, Shoshanah Nisanov and her son Yehezkel immigrated to Palestine after another one of her sons, Yehudah, was killed by Muslims while defending Jews in the city of Temir-Khan-Shurah. Two years later, her son Zvi also joined them, and both sons became members of Ha-Shomer. The family lived in Masha (Kefar Tabor), and Shoshanah's house was a warm, friendly place always open to members of the group. Her two sons carried out guard duty for the organization and were known for their audacity. Yehezkel Nisanov was killed on February 23, 1911, in an ambush. Shoshanah urged her son Zvi to avenge his brother's death (an accepted practice in the Caucasus), but his friends in Ha-Shomer persuaded him not to do so.

Theodor Herzl with delegates of the community of Mountain Jews at the Fourth Zionist Congress, Basel, 1900
Photo courtesy of the Central Zionist Archives, Jerusalem

אגודת צעירים ההרים ארץ־ישׂ

Caucasian immigration to Palestine continued in a trickle following World War I. Approximately 1,000 people requested to immigrate to Palestine in 1922. They arrived in Istanbul and wandered among the various organizations there, hungry and without any documents. Michael Abramov, the group's representative, traveled to Palestine on numerous occasions, each time only succeeding in attaining an aliyah permit for several dozen families. A total of 175 families received such permits. In 1926, 126 families immigrated to Palestine, some traversing Iran and Iraq by foot and arriving penniless. For a short time, some of the families lived in tents on the beach of Tel Aviv. In 1924, a Caucasian quarter was established in Tel Aviv; it was torn down sixty years later when the new central bus station was built. Yekutiel Adam, a general in the Israel Defence Forces who was killed in the Lebanon War in 1982, was the most celebrated member of this group of Caucasian immigrants.

In 1926, the settlement of Kefar Baruch, located near Nahalal in the Jezreel Valley, was established by a group of families from Bulgaria, Kurdistan, Turkey, and the Caucasus. At first, there were no roads leading to the settlement and no water supply, and the settlers lived in tents. More than half of the settlers who remained there two years later were Caucasian immigrants. Shaul Rabaiov, an experienced farmer and popular public activist, was the most prominent personality in the village. His sons followed in his footsteps and held senior positions in the Jewish Brigade, and later in the IDF.

Members of the Organization of Young Mountain Jews in Palestine protest against the government's decision not to draft them into the British Border Police, Tel Aviv, 1929
Photo courtesy of Beth Hatefutsoth, The Nahum Goldmann Museum of the Jewish Diaspora, Tel Aviv

The Immigration of the 1970s and 1990s

An important aliyah arrived from the Caucasus in the 1970s, and in June 1981, seventy families established the settlement of Hinnanit on the hills overlooking Wadi 'Ara. Another major wave of immigration arrived during the 1990s, and by the end of that decade the Caucasian community in Israel numbered about 80,000 persons. They are dispersed throughout Israel, and live mainly in Acre, the North Sharon area – Or Akiva, Hadera, Pardes Hannah – and, in the south, in Beersheva, Ofakim, and Sderot.

Mountain Jews say *kaddish* (prayer for the dead) in the cemetery on the Mount of Olives, Jerusalem, 1906
Photo courtesy of Moshe Yosifov, Jerusalem

The physician Dr. Aharon
Binyamini (1887–1943)
(left), who was actively
involved in public affairs
and especially in Mountain
Jewish organizations
Photo courtesy of Arnon Itzhaki,
Be'er Ya'akov

Central Organization
of the
CAUCASIAN MOUNTAIN - JEWS
in JERUSALEM (Eretz-Israel)

מרכז הסתדרות
היהודים ההרריים הקוקזים
בירושלם א"י

№ ....   Jerusalem 17 . 9 . 35 . ב"ה ירושלם י"ם אלול חרצ"ה

ה צ ה ר ה

אנחנו החו"מ שכונת בית ישראל ושכונה רחובות הבוכארים , מעידים על החצר שנמצא

בשכונתנו שנקרא קהלת הקוקזים , זה קרוב לחמש ועשרים שנים שקנה אותו ח' פסח

פבאיוב עם שותפו ת' יאודא בר יוסף מזקנים וזקנות אוסף נדחים בית גדול 10 מטר

ומגרש שלפניו , מיום שקנה נתן הבית לקהלת הקוקזים בחזר בית הכנסת עד ה"יום ,

ומתפללים בו הקהל וגם נבנה ארבעת חדרים במגרש על יד בית הכנסת על ידי המנוח

הרב ר' יעקב יצחק' רב של הקהלה , וגם קנה הרב יעקב יצחק' מאת וחמשים (150)

אמות קרקע מהמנוח יעקב מאגיר   עבד בנין של ארבעת חדרים כפי התבנית , וארבעת

חדרים חדשים שכר באי כח פבאיוב אחרי המלחמה לחמשה שנים רצופים , וקבלו את כל

השכירות ולא ראינו ולא שמענו שיום אדם מפריע אותם , ולראיה באנו על החתם

פה עיר הקודש ירושלים ח"ו ביום חנז"ל

1. משה בן רב' יוסף

Pioneers building roads in
Palestine, 1925
Photo courtesy of Beth Hatefutsoth,
The Nahum Goldmann Museum of
the Jewish Diaspora, Tel Aviv

Founders of the Be'er
Ya'akov settlement, 1908
Photo courtesy of Beth Hatefutsoth,
The Nahum Goldmann Museum of
the Jewish Diaspora, Tel Aviv

וֶסֶב , ... סלות כפי הצורך .

וֶסִית , נוזאה לגזוה זאת לפני וזתן . ...

וֶסָל , ע/ן האוניה באוב . ונראו סל הל אוב , ורנוסל
עליו ... הווניה הנבבא יורה כ/ ... וכ א הלוב , התנמות
הלוב , וזובב .

וֶסְרִי , בית יד של ונכול .

וֶצָה , ע/ן ריקוד . ונראה צה , ל'ל קפיבה וזקום נבוה לוקום
וזוך . והוא וָנְסֶרָא , ונאור עריותו כפאל צה .

וֶצֶק , פחב , איאה , וצוה .

וֶצַ , ע/ן אסיפה וקיבול הדברים הזפוריים . והוא וָנֶּרָא
באע/ן אחר קוף , וַצ , כתיבה והעתקה וסכר אל סכר .

וֶצֵר , ע/ן הריסה והיפוק .

וֶצָא , אפרוח הצוף . והואול לשאר קטב בעה להקטוב .

וִיצֵא , וֶרֶד .

וֶצַן , ע/ן הרירה ובחירה .

Language and Literature
Michael Zand

The language spoken by Mountain Jews is an ethnolect of Tat, which belongs to the southwestern subgroup of the Iranian languages. Four local dialects of this ethnolect can be identified: those of Derbent, Kuba, Makhachkala-Nalchik (historically, the Haytaghi dialect), and Vartashen – now Oguz (historically, the Shirvani dialect). The usual designation for this ethnolect in the scientific literature is "Judeo-Tat," but the Mountain Jews call it *zuhun juhuri** – literally, "the Jewish language." Dialects of Tat (as distinct from Judeo-Tat) are spoken by some Muslims in Azerbaijan and by a small Christian group that recently emigrated from there to Armenia.

From time immemorial, Hebrew was the dominant written language of Mountain Jews. During the seventeenth and eighteenth centuries, Hebrew religious literature flourished. In the early nineteenth century, Mattityahu Ha-Kohen Mizrahi of Shemakha wrote a kabbalistic work in Hebrew entitled *Kol Mevasser*. At the beginning of the twentieth century, Rabbi Yosef ben Hayyim Shor (who died after 1921) wrote Hebrew verse in the style of Yehudah Halevi, imbued with longing for Zion.

As far as we know, the first written document relating to the Judeo-Tat language was *Otzar ha-Millim shel ha-Safah ha-Tatit-Yehudit* (A Lexicon of Judeo-Tat), compiled in the 1870s and 1880s by Rabbi Ya'akov Itzhakovich-Yitzhaki (1848–1917). It contains nearly 1,900 words in the Derbent dialect with their Hebrew translation. The first book printed in Judeo-Tat, Asaf Pinhasov's translation of a Russian work by Yosef Sapir (1869–1935), appeared in Vilna in 1908 as *Metleb Siyoniho* (The Aim of Zionists). A year later, also in Vilna, Pinhasov issued a prayer book with Judeo-Tat translation. Between 1915 and 1922, three Judeo-Tat newspapers were published in Baku, but they were short-lived, running only to a few issues. The first Judeo-Tat primer appeared in Baku during the early 1920s.

From 1927, the city of Derbent in Dagestan became the focus of Judeo-Tat activity. At the national conference on Caucasian Jewish culture held in Moscow that same year, it was resolved that the Judeo-Tat literary language should be based on the Derbent dialect. *Zehmetkesh* (The Laborer), a newspaper published in Derbent in 1928–41, played a substantial part in further strengthening the status of the Derbent dialect. Alongside Judeo-Tat publications printed in the Hebrew alphabet, with additional diacritics traditionally used for writing in Judeo-Tat, others appeared in 1927–28 using two "improved" versions of the Hebrew alphabet with different vocalization systems to furnish the missing vowels. In 1929, following a government decision of the previous year, Hebrew was replaced by the Latin alphabet, and it took another year to fully implement this measure. The Judeo-Tat grammar published by Naftali Zvi Anisimov in Moscow in 1932 remains the only work of its type. Latin finally gave way to the Russian Cyrillic alphabet in1938, and Judeo-Tat has been written in that form ever since.

Many works in Judeo-Tat appeared during the years 1930–37, and it became the language of instruction in a growing number of schools. In 1938, the autonomous republic of Dagestan made Tat (as it was called) one of its ten official languages. From that year on, however, the number of publications in Judeo-Tat dwindled considerably.

* The transliteration of Judeo-Tat terms in this article is by Michael Zand.

Opposite:
Page from *A Lexicon of Judeo-Tat*, compiled by Rabbi Ya'akov Yitzhaki, Derbent, Dagestan, 1870–80
Lent by the Ben-Zvi Institute, Jerusalem

Evening class in a Jewish
school established by
Shaul Bar-Avrum, Derbent,
Dagestan, 1925
Photo courtesy of the Shaul
Bar-Avrum family, Derbent,
Dagestan

From 1938, Russian began to replace Judeo-Tat as the language of instruction in Dagestan's Jewish
schools, while Azerbaijani and/or Russian did so in Azerbaijan's. A professional theater established in
Derbent in 1935 gave fortnightly performances of dramas and musicals in Judeo-Tat, but it was closed
eleven years later on the pretext that its shows were of no interest to theatergoers. Neither the few
amateur companies that later performed once in a while at collective farms (kolkhozes) of Mountain
Jews, nor the "Inter-Kolkhoz Tat Theater" (renamed "Tat People's Theater" in 1966), which also made
sporadic appearances, attained the high standard of the professional theater.

For centuries, the Mountain Jews were characterized by bilingualism. In Azerbaijan and southern
Dagestan they spoke Judeo-Tat and Azerbaijani, in northern Dagestan – Judeo-Tat and Qumiq. From
the late 1920s, particularly during the 1930s, Russian started to replace Azerbaijani and Qumiq.
Publication of works in Judeo-Tat was suspended altogether during the war between Soviet Russia and
Nazi Germany (1941–45), and was only renewed in 1946, when a few political pamphlets, translated
from Russian, made their appearance. From the late 1940s until the 1990s, two or three books a year
were published on the average. One of these was a slim almanac entitled *Vatan Sovetimu* (Our Soviet
Homeland), which appeared during the years 1960–91; another was a propagandist work translated

from Russian. The ending of instruction in Judeo-Tat and the wartime suspension of publication in this language (only renewed on the most limited scale) hastened the Mountain Jews' transition to Russian as their main or even only language.

The literature written in Judeo-Tat was preceded by a rich and creative folklore that comprised mainly folktales (*ovosune*), poems (*me'ni*), and proverbs (*metele*). The tales were, for the most part, related by professional storytellers (*ovosunechi*). Some of the verse was composed by well-known folk poets and, as the lines were recited, the author's name was usually mentioned. The genres in which women specialized were lullabies (*nenem-nenuy*) and funeral songs (known as *girye* in Azerbaijan and southern Dagestan and as *domoyos* in northern Dagestan and the northern Caucasus).

Plays staged in Derbent's Jewish school at the beginning of the twentieth century may be seen as an early attempt to produce literary work in Judeo-Tat. During the 1920s, when the Mountain Jews established their literature, stage plays won the highest regard. They were mostly the work of actors belonging to amateur companies. The most popular plays of that time were by Yona Semyonov (1899–1961), a founder of the Derbent amateur troupe, who also wrote poems and stories. In the plays of the 1920s one can detect the influence of the Azerbaijani dramatic school:

Boys in a traditional Jewish school (*nubokhunde*), Kuba, Azerbaijan, ca. 1920
Photo courtesy of Beth Hatefutsoth, The Nahum Goldmann Museum of the Jewish Diaspora, Tel Aviv

"Basic Education," a Jewish
theater troupe formed to
promote Russian music and
language among the
Mountain Jews, Nalchik,
Kabardino-Balkaria, 1930s
Photo courtesy of Svetlana
Danilova, Nalchik

a one-dimensional plot structure, simple or even shallow characterization of the figures, and an abundance of musical items worked into the play.

Semyonov also made an important contribution to the dramatic literature of the 1930s. *Du biror* (Two Brothers), a play dating from about 1930, reflects the grim conflict besetting a village of Mountain Jews, where the traditional way of life clashed with the new lifestyle of Soviet Russia. During the late 1930s, Mishi (Moshe) Bakhshiyev (1910–1972) was the outstanding playwright. *Besghuni igidho* (Victory of the Heroes, 1936), his portrayal of the Civil War era in Dagestan, was the first heroic drama in the Mountain Jews' literature. Another of Bakhshiyev's plays, *Khuri* (Earth, 1939), shows how the kolkhozes of the Mountain Jews were merged with non-Jewish collective farms. This Sovietization measure, which, alongside its economic aspects, hastened the destruction of traditional life among Jews and non-Jews alike, is depicted in line with Communist ideology as a welcome step towards "the brotherhood of peoples."

With the closure of the Mountain Jewish professional theater in 1946 (see above), there was a sharp decline in new output in the field of drama. In general, the few plays written thereafter were aesthetically inferior to those of the 1930s. Two notable exceptions were Bakhshiyev's psychological drama *Du dedey* (Two Mothers, 1965), which deals with the conflict between a natural and an adoptive

mother (and expresses Bakhshiyev's unfettered admiration for the latter), and Semyon (Shimon) Yusufov's *Jufde parusdekho* (A Pair of Swallows, 1971), which portrays Jewish life in Dagestan at the time.

Regular publication of original verse only began in 1928, with the appearance of the aforementioned *Zehmetkesh* newspaper. During the 1920s, poets dealt with contemporary themes on two planes: daily life among the Jews and, more broadly, in Dagestan or Soviet Russia as a whole. During the 1930s, poetry became the dominant genre of Judeo-Tat literature, with young writers who had grown up in the Soviet era taking the lead. Emphasis was placed on changes that had occurred in the lifestyle of Mountain Jews, and this often found expression in poems devoted to the status of women. A notable example was *Du koghoz* (Two Letters, 1934) by Monuvah (Manoah) Dadashev (1913–1943), which displays genuine lyricism and an effort to delineate the psychological portraits of its heroes despite the ideological clichés typical of the poetry of the era. Verse structure was then characterized by a gradual transition from metrical and rhyme patterns of folkloric origin to others borrowed from Russian poetry.

The imprisonment of several writers during Stalin's Great Purges (1936–38) dealt a savage blow to the literature of the Mountain Jews. All but one of the detainees perished in jail or in "corrective labor camps." During the Second World War, most Mountain Jewish writers were enlisted in the Red Army and two of them – Monuvah Dadashev and Ya'akov Birorov – died at the front.

Hed Harim (Mountain Echo), a Zionist newspaper published by the Central Committee of Mountain Jews; printed in Judeo-Tat in Hebrew script; Baku, Azerbaijan, 1920
Lent by Leah Shapira, Beersheva

Danil (Daniel) Atnilov (1915–1968), who embarked on his literary career in the late 1930s, became the best-known and most prolific writer of the postwar era from among the Mountain Jews. As a permanent resident in Moscow, cut off from his Judeo-Tat mother tongue, Atnilov developed a rare feeling for the language. He had an urge to display all of its richness and to use words (including Hebrew ones) that rarely occur in daily speech. His works bear the stamp of contemporary Russian writers who sought and fashioned new modes of poetic expression. They also contain a good deal of free verse and deliberately imperfect rhyme.

During the 1960s, prompted by his remoteness from the daily life of Mountain Jews, Atnilov became the first to publish verse which asserted that Mountain Jews did not belong to the Jewish people, but constituted a separate ethnic group – the Tat people. During the 1970s and 1980s, faithful to the "Tat line" that Atnilov had pioneered in Mountain Jewish literature, other works appeared (including narrative prose, poems, and essays), especially journalistic essays, expressing a negative stance towards Israel and aliyah (immigration to Israel). Even in these, however, the claim that Mountain Jews are distinct from the Jewish people is paradoxically combined with an emotional acknowledgment of their Jewishness.

The earliest prose written by Mountain Jews also dates from the late 1920s, and Yona Semyonov (mentioned earlier) was among the pioneers in this field too. One task that Communist ideologues assigned to literature throughout the Soviet Union was the campaign against religion. This ideological task is performed by Semyonov's lengthy tale, *Oshnehoy en rabi Hesdil* (Rabbi Hesdil's Paramours, 1928), in which a Mountain Jewish rabbi is caricatured as a swindler, chronic drunkard, and incorrigible womanizer. Two novellas by Mishi Bakhshiyev achieved prominence in the early 1930s: *E pushorehi toze zindeguni* (Towards a New Life, 1932) deals with the period before and just after the Revolution; *Vetegechiho* (The Fishermen, 1933), a portrayal of Derbent Jews who earned their livelihood from fishing in the Caspian, is notable for its skillful plot and characterization. During the late 1930s, Hizghil (Yehezkel) Avshalumov (1913–2001) published his first stories and essays while Hizghil Dadashev (1860–1944), a professional storyteller, combined themes drawn from Soviet life with a narrative style rooted in folklore.

On their return to Dagestan in the early 1950s, after a long period of military service, Bakhshiyev and Avshalumov started to write fiction in both Russian and Judeo-Tat. The first works published after his homecoming show that Bakhshiyev tried to serve as an all-Dagestani writer, not limiting himself to Jewish motifs. However, in the novel entitled *Khushehoy ongur* (Clusters of Grapes, 1963), virtually all the action takes place among the Mountain Jews. This was the first attempt by any Mountain Jewish writer to produce a multilayered novel. While its plot is that of a typical "Kolkhoz novel" (engendered by Soviet literature of the late 1950s and early 1960s), the subplot of a family romance is woven into it — as is a clearly anti-Stalinist line. Though Bakhshiyev's handling of the latter issue is hesitant, the fact that he deals with it at all is a rare phenomenon in Mountain Jewish writing of the period.

General Dagestani themes also loom large in the works of Avshalumov, and he devotes many of them to figures of his time. Nevertheless, his best works hark back to the days when the Mountain Jews' traditional lifestyle was shattered. In his novella *Zenbiror* (The Sister-in-Law, 1971), Avshalumov

Selected poems by Ilyas
Nizami (1141–1209; lived
in Azerbaijan, wrote in
Persian), published in
Judeo-Tat translation in
Cyrillic script, Baku,
Azerbaijan, 1940
Lent by Haim Agarunov, Hadera

Леонид Ильич БРЕЖНЕВ

ЧУЬКЛЕ ХОРИ

ТОЗЕДЕН ОВОДУ СОХДЕ ОМОРЕ

Malaya Zemlya and
The Revival by Leonid
Brezhnev, published in
Judeo-Tat translation in
Cyrillic script, Makhachkala,
Dagestan, 1978
Lent by Haim Agarunov, Hadera

A Mountain Jewish theater
troupe, Kuba, Azerbaijan,
1930s
Photo courtesy of Haim Agarunov,
Hadera

portrays the life of Derbent Jewry's social elite on the eve of the Revolution and the 1917–21 Civil War, throughout that period, and during the Soviet regime's consolidation in the early 1920s. The same era is mirrored in his *Kuk gudil* (The Jester's Son, 1974), a novella outstanding for its ethnographically accurate portrayal of the Mountain Jewish farmer's attire, home, labor, mode of conduct, and usual pastimes before the Revolution. The various characters that figure in this work are delineated with great precision, offering the reader a mosaic of Jewish village life in Dagestan prior to the Soviet regime. The novella's two key elements stand in direct contradiction to each other. One is emotional, namely, the author's deep, subconscious nostalgia for what was once and is no more – the traditional collective of Mountain Jews that maintained itself as a self-contained ethnic entity. The other is ideological, impelling the author to compose a Mountain Jewish epic narrative on the Soviet Russian pattern, with the aim of glorifying a revolution that destroyed the very characters that he portrayed with such impressive artistry.

Elements of folkloric origin are distinctly visible in Avshalumov's collection of humorous and satirical short stories, *Shimi Derbendi* (Shimi of Derbent, 1978), the eponymous hero being a penniless Jew who radiates joie de vivre. Avshalumov's greatest work in Russian was *Tolmach imama* (The Imam's Interpreter, 1967). The hero of this novella is a Russian soldier acting as an interpreter for Shamil, the imam who led the great Caucasian revolt against the Russians in 1834–59.

Only during the 1960s did a growing number of writers start to produce works in Russian. They include, among others, the poet Lazar Amirov (born in 1936; immigrated to Israel in 1995); the prose writer Felix Bakhshiyev (born in 1938); and the poet and essayist Roman Badalov (born in 1941; immigrated to Israel in 1995). Boris Hanukayev (born in 1952; immigrated to Israel in 1991) and Aleksey Yakobov (born in 1929; immigrated to Israel in 1996) have authored works in both Russian and Judeo-Tat.

During the 1990s, in the wake of the mass immigration of Mountain Jews to Israel, many writers also settled in Israel, and a Union of Mountain Jewish Writers was established in 1999. Most of those who joined it have already published works here and continue to do so.

Pedazur Ashurov (1926–2000), dancer and musician in the Kabardina troupe, Nalchik, Kabardino-Balkaria
Photo courtesy of the Ashurov family, Beersheva

Religion
and Tradition

Crown, Quill, and Crest: Torah Finials and Pointers in Azerbaijan and Dagestan
Ariella Amar

The Torah finials (*rimmonim*) and pointers (*yadayim*) of the Mountain Jews shed light on their cultural and visual world.[1] It transpires that this community has a rich visual tradition that distinguishes it from other Jewish communities while testifying to a link with neighboring peoples.

Owing to their reduced circumstances, the Mountain Jews seem initially not to have possessed many objects. As a result of historical events – the Caucasian peoples' revolt against Russian subjugation (1834–59) and the Bolshevik Revolution (1917) – little of their meager patrimony survived.[2] Apart from Torah cases dating from 1950 onwards, the small number of ritual objects that are extant mostly date from the early nineteenth to the first half of the twentieth century. This chapter focuses on the Mountain Jews' finials and pointers, which are shown to display a connection with the Persian cultural environment, bordering on Azerbaijan to the south, and with Georgia, which lies immediately to the northwest of the regions studied here.

Torah Finials

The Torah finials examined in various synagogues of Derbent (Dagestan), Kuba and Baku (Azerbaijan) provide evidence of a consolidated visual tradition that is expressed in their shape and ornamentation and in the inscriptions engraved on them. This tradition persisted for at least 150 years – from the earliest pair of finials known so far (1812) to the most recent example (1957). Though generally similar in their shape, these finials can be divided into five main groups, which are presented below in chronological order.

The first group, the earliest, is represented by a single pair of finials dating from 1812 (fig. 1, over) and dedicated by Hivat bar Noah. The body of each is globular, with a cylindrical crest surmounted by a dome. Chains with spherical bells hang from the top of the crest and the middle of the body. A short, narrow shaft supports the body of the finials, which is adorned by a circular pattern of vertical cartouches enclosing floral motifs and an inscription. Engraved within and between the cartouches is the biblical verse describing the ornamented hem of the High Priest's robe: "A golden bell and a pomegranate, a golden bell and a pomegranate, upon the hem of the robe round about" (Exodus 28:34), accompanied by a dedicatory inscription.

The second group comprises a set of finials produced between 1817 and 1859 (see fig. 2, over). These resemble the previous group in their shape and components, apart from an encircling horizontal band that divides the spherical body in half. Two of these finials originated in Derbent and, unlike the other finials in this group, their inscriptions are enclosed in rhombuses rather than in oval cartouches (Sc-472-2).[3]

The third group comprises a collection of finials produced between 1847 and 1920. These have an elliptical body made of two hemispheres joined together in the middle by a wide encircling band (fig. 3, over). At the top of the body is a cylindrical crest surmounted by a dome. This dome was

Opposite:
Torah ark in the Gilah synagogue with Torah scrolls wrapped in typical Caucasian fashion, with three layers: first a mantle of white cotton (called *zir-shey brusi* meaning "bride's underdress"); then a mantle of red velvet (called *gobo ḥatoni*, meaning bridegroom's coat); and on top of these a colorful scarf. Kuba, Azerbaijan
Photo taken in 1996

1

2

3

1. Torah finials, 1812
Silver, repoussé and
engraved, with glass inlay
H 24.5
Sc-475-11

2. Torah finial, Azerbaijan,
1817
Silver, repoussé and
engraved
H 30
Sc-473-10

3. Toral finial, Kubachi,
Dagestan, 1847
Silver, repoussé and
engraved
H 28
Sc-473-9

Photos courtesy of the Center for
Jewish Art, The Hebrew University
of Jerusalem

sometimes topped by a large apex in the shape of a star enclosing a crescent (*illal* in Arabic). The ornamentation of these finials is similar to that of the groups previously described, except for two examples which feature only inscriptions and no ornamentation. Most of the finials were crafted by a highly proficient silversmith. Like the two previous groups, these have inscriptions engraved in cartouches – but they also display the forty-two-letter Name of God, an acrostic based on the initial letters of *Anna be-Kho'ah*, a prayer ascribed to R. Nehunya ben Ha-Kanah, which is thought to possess magical powers.[4]

The fourth group is represented by a single pair of finials, lacking a date, which have unusual components and ornamentation (see illustration on p. 54). They are composed of a spherical body and conical base supported by a long shaft with a rounded capital at the top. Surmounting the body is a small apex in the shape of a coronet with a pointed prism in the middle. The finial's body is adorned with a figure riding a horse and with additional animal figures, while the base and capital have a geometric decoration.

The fifth group comprises a set of finials dating from the first half of the twentieth century. Although their shape and components resemble those of the second group, the composition of the inscriptions and ornamentation differs. The body of each finial is decorated with horizontal encircling bands which alternately contain inscriptions and black niello strips (see ill. on p. 53, left). In addition to the biblical phrase about the High Priest's robe mentioned in relation to the first group of finials, the names of Jacob's sons also feature on these finials. The order in which they appear varies from one finial to another – sometimes in accordance with their order of birth, as set forth in Jacob's blessing (Genesis 49), and at other times according to their respective mothers (Genesis 35:23–26).

Short and narrow cylindrical shafts are a unique feature of most Caucasian finials. These narrow shafts did not match the thicker Torah staves, and, to make them fit, an improvised layer of base material was added to each shaft (see figs. 1, 2, and 3). A similar phenomenon is visible in another finial, belonging to the Caucasian group but dedicated in 1872 to the Jewish community of Carmina, Uzbekistan (Sc-229-6). This single example resembles the Caucasian finials in shape and ornamentation; in 1919, a long shaft was added to the short, narrow one at its base, as was done with other Caucasian finials.

Information about ceremonial objects and their utilization by the Mountain Jews before and during the nineteenth century is very scarce. Community elders do not recall that finials were placed on Torah staves and maintain that this custom is relatively recent. When interviewed, however, they were unable to describe any other practice involving finials. According to their tradition, the use of finials was introduced to the Caucasus by a Persian Jew of the Cohen family, originally from Tabriz in western Persia, who escaped from the Shirvan district of southern Azerbaijan after an earthquake in 1812 and took refuge in Baku, bringing with him a pair of finials. Whether this folktale has any historical basis remains uncertain, but it may reflect a situation in which the use of finials was not prevalent.[5]

It is possible that members of the Jewish community were provided by local silversmiths with artifacts that they had available, whose shape recalled the visual tradition of finials with which Mountain Jews were familiar, and which were then adapted for use as Torah finials. Objects resembling these finials in shape and ornamentation are used by Muslim inhabitants of the region. Thus, for example, banners carried in Islamic processions are adorned with finials which have a spherical body encircled by chains with bells and topped by a large apex (see ill. above, right). What provides a striking resemblance between the finials of these Muslim banners and the Torah finials is the short shaft fixed at their base, which makes it possible to fit them onto flagpoles.

Metal objects in the region were mostly produced by Muslim craftsmen, and few Jews are known to have engaged in this trade. One major center in the eastern Caucasus, particularly for the silversmith's craft, is southern Dagestan. This center provided various parts of Dagestan and

Left: Torah finial, Kubachi, Dagestan, 1911
Silver, repoussé and engraved, with niello inlay
H 17.5
Sc-477-4
Photos courtesy of the Center for Jewish Art, The Hebrew University of Jerusalem

Right: Spherical finials adorning banners carried in Islamic processions, 19th century
Photo from Tuyakbayeva, *Epigraphic Decorations*, p. 18

Torah finials, Majalis,
Dagestan, 19th century
Silver, repoussé, embossed,
and engraved, with niello
H 29.8
Lent by the Gross family, Tel Aviv

Azerbaijan with metal (notably silver) articles, and the town of Kubachi in southern Dagestan was particularly renowned for the niello technique of its silversmiths. A comparison between everyday items produced in Kubachi and the Torah finials reveals that they share a common style and visual tradition. Thus, for example, the composition of the decorations on a silver cap worn by women (see ill. on p. 60) and their disposition at regular intervals recall the composition of the motifs adorning the pair of finials dating from 1918 (see ill. on p. 56).

In these same finials, the large apex composed of a crescent enclosing a six-pointed star – an emblem that derives from the Ottoman empire – also bears witness to the Muslim environment in which these items were produced. The closest examples of such apexes appear in pendants decorated with thin niello strips that originate in Kubachi. The Torah finials were undoubtedly produced by one of that town's finest silversmiths, whose craftsmanship is manifest in the skillful design and precise niello work. The Torah finial from Carmina (Sc-229-6) and the finials of the fifth group may also have been made in Kubachi. A similar style and ornamentation can be found in various local artifacts, especially jewelry.

Other silversmiths practiced their trade in Baku and Derbent. Most of the finials of the second group were probably produced in Baku, though further research is needed to ascertain this. Two pairs of this group, dating from 1859, were very likely made in Derbent (Sc-477-2). Their linear and geometric style of decoration, unlike that of other finials in this group, was apparently the work of an amateur silversmith. The plainness of their ornamentation may also attest to the inferior economic status of the Derbent Jews and their inability to acquire expensive, high-quality silver goods. Linear, geometric ornamentation can also be found in the finial of the fourth group (see ill. on p. 54), which was dedicated by two members of the Jewish community in Majalis, a town located about forty kilometers west of Derbent. The finial's body is decorated with unusual motifs – a horse and rider, a lion (?), and a leopard (?).[6] These schematic, linear motifs are reminiscent of the carpets manufactured in the Shirvan region of southern Azerbaijan. Without a sufficient number of articles from other towns to facilitate a comparison, it is hard to determine where the remaining finials were produced.

Torah finials, Baku,
Azerbaijan, 1908
Silver, repoussé and
engraved
H 34
Sc-473-1
Photo courtesy of the Center for
Jewish Art, The Hebrew University
of Jerusalem

Torah finials
Kubachi, Dagestan, 1918
Silver, repoussé , cast, and
engraved, with niello and
glass inlay
H 43
Sc-473-2
Photo courtesy of the Center for
Jewish Art, The Hebrew University
of Jerusalem

Side by side with environmental influences on the design of the shape and ornamentation of the finials, it is also possible to detect the influence of Jewish tradition, mainly from Persia. Until the Russians occupied eastern Caucasia in the nineteenth century, the Mountain Jews – like the Jews of Bukhara and Afghanistan – formed part of the Persian cultural environment.[7] Evidence of this link with Persia's Jewish communities may be found in a pair of finials of the Georgian type (see ill. on p. 55), on which the following inscription is engraved: "These finials were dedicated in the house of our God by the Sephardi community, the holy congregation of Persia in [B]aku . . . in the year 5668 [1908]." The Sephardim who donated these finials were thus Persian Jews who had established a congregation in Baku. Whereas most other finials were produced in Muslim workshops, the shape, decoration, engraved inscriptions, and names on this specific pair attest to a close connection with Persian Jewry.

Most of the finials used by Mountain Jews are called *keter Torah* (Torah crown), a designation also known in Persia and Afghanistan.[8] There is no certainty as to the origin of this term, which may derive from a passage in the Mishnah (Avot 4:13), where *keter Torah* is mentioned as one of four honorific titles bestowed upon distinguished persons.[9] "Torah crown" was the name given metaphorically to any sacred ornament placed on top of the Torah scroll. Its unusual use as denoting finials derives from this understanding of *keter Torah* as an overall term, together with the fact that the Mountain Jews did not place any other ornaments on top of the Torah scrolls. Like most other Eastern communities, the Mountain Jews followed the practice of keeping their scrolls in flat-topped wooden cases that resembled one of the types used in Persia, Bukhara, and Afghanistan, with finials rather than a crown surmounting them.[10]

Caucasian finials resemble one of the Persian types of finials not only in their name but also in their shape and components.[11] Those from Isfahan in Persia have a spherical body from which a cylindrical crest emerges, topped by a cupola (see ill. on p. 57) – but, unlike Caucasian finials, the body and crest usually form a single unit, giving them a pear-shaped appearance. This unity is reflected in the decoration of the cartouches and the arrangement of branches over the finial's surface. The way these cartouches are set in a decorative band around the middle resembles that of the Hivat bar Noah finial from 1812, and this pattern can also be found in the early finials of the second group and in some of the third group. Despite their similar shape and common motifs, however, there are stylistic differences between Caucasian and Persian finials. The Isfahan finials have flowing lines of twisted branches that create a sense of movement, whereas the lines in the Caucasian finials produce a rigid and less condensed effect than those in the Isfahan examples. The decorative technique also differs: the finials from Isfahan have an engraved ornamentation, whereas the Caucasian examples are partly ornamented in niello, a technique that emphasizes the black areas and contour lines, which are generally thicker. One should therefore not assume that there is any direct connection between the two types of finials; rather, the resemblance in their shape and components may indicate that the finials from the Isfahan region and the Caucasian ones were based on a common model. That putative model could also have influenced the design of finials in other Jewish communities within Persia's cultural sphere (Bukhara and Afghanistan), even if each area developed its own particular characteristics, which are mainly visible in the different proportions and ornamental style.[12]

As stated previously, four of the five groups of finials are inscribed with a verse from Exodus (see p. 51). This verse is also engraved on most finials of Georgian origin. There were commercial and cultural ties between the Georgian and the Mountain Jews, and communities were even established by the former in cities of Eastern Caucasia. There is no certainty as to how and when this verse began to be used on finials. The oldest extant Caucasian finial on which the verse appears dates from 1812 (the Hivat bar Noah example), while the earliest Georgian example recorded dates only from 1859.[13] The appearance of this verse on both may attest to a tradition shared by the communities of Georgia and Eastern Caucasia, or to the influence that one of these communities exerted on the other.

Reciprocal relations between the two communities and the influence of the Georgian visual tradition on its neighbor to the east can also be seen in the pair of finials from 1908, which (as mentioned earlier) the "holy congregation of Persia" dedicated in Baku (see ill. on p. 55). Their tower-like shape, comprising a hexagonal body surmounted by a dome, reflects the design of the Georgian type of finials, and they feature similar inscriptions.[14] Each of the sides bears an engraving of the verse from Exodus as well as the following passages: "This is the Torah which Moses set before the children of Israel; these are the testimonies and the statutes . . ." (Deuteronomy 4:44–45); the Priestly Blessing (Numbers 6:24–27); and the Ten Commandments (Exodus 20:2–14). Alongside the traditional Georgian inscriptions, the Persian community also added the forty-two-letter Name of God that adorns the finials of the third group. This Divine Name, to which amuletic powers are traditionally ascribed, is found on Persian finials and amulets, but not on the finials made in Georgia for the indigenous community.[15]

Torah finals, Isfahan, Persia, 1965
Silver, repoussé
H 35
Sc.Ka.Be.Y.3
Photo courtesy of the Center for Jewish Art, The Hebrew University of Jerusalem

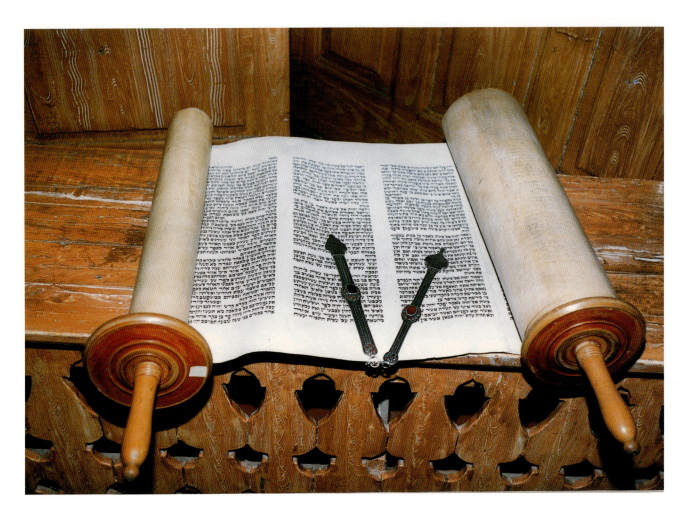

Pointers

Perhaps the most striking feature of Caucasian pointers is the way they were used — held in pairs in the shape of a "V" so as to divide the recitation into short passages. Under the influence of the Russian Ashkenazi community, this distinctive custom (illustrated above, as reconstructed with the help of community elders), became less widespread. The pointers were made and donated in pairs or joined together when their dedicatory inscriptions related to the same event; the end held when reading the Torah has a ring inserted with a chain fastened to it, permitting the attachment of the other pointer. This arrangement is not always adhered to nowadays and the pointers are sometimes combined in random pairs (see, for example, Sc-474-23, 24).

The large collection of Caucasian pointers can be divided into two main types, according to their shape: some are flat while others consist of a twisted bar (see figs. A and B). In both types the indicating section is formed of a broad, flat leaf with wavy edges culminating in a rounded tip. Both types of pointers reflect separate visual traditions that coexisted for more than a century, beginning with the early example of 1819 and extending to the one made in 1959. The example of the first type (fig. A) bears witness to a local tradition that continued throughout that period. The middle of this pointer and the end held by the reader are enlarged and inlaid with multicolored stones or

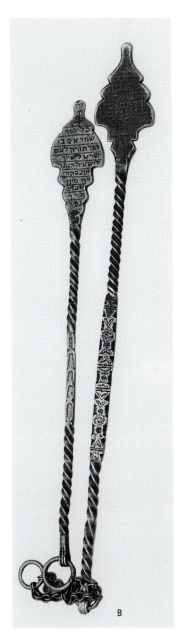

glass, creating the shape of an open flower with a large stone in the center and smaller ones around it. Silver bands composed of tiny balls set in a row frame the edges of the pointer and occasionally spread over the bar's entire surface. Its flat structure, together with the components and extent of its ornamentation, resemble those of bracelets from southern Dagestan (see ill. above, right). Such distinctive bracelets formed part of the traditional dress of women in the villages of Naktil, Urda, and Tidib. The style, composition, and techniques shared by those bracelets and the Torah pointers may indicate that they had a common local visual tradition, one apparently forged by the same craftsmen in southern Dagestan. Unlike the finals, however, these pointers seem to have been specifically designed for reading the Torah.

A. Torah pointers, southern Dagestan, 1830
Silver, engraved and soldered, inlaid with precious stones
L 26.5
Sc-474-40
Photo courtesy of the Center for Jewish Art, The Hebrew University of Jerusalem

B. Torah pointers, Kuba, Azerbaijan, 1860; 1873
L 37.5
Photo courtesy of the Center for Jewish Art, The Hebrew University of Jerusalem

Woman's bracelet, southern Dagestan, early 19th century
Silver, repoussé and inlaid
Photograph from Chirov, *Daghestan Decorative Art*, p. 120

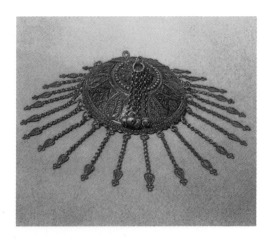

Woman's skullcap, Kubachi, Dagestan, early 20th century
Silver with niello and filigree
Photograph from Razina, Cherkasova, and Kantsedikas, *Folk Art*, p. 167

Pointers of the second type, fashioned between the year 1860 and 1924, mainly consist of three sections: two twisted ends with a four-sided bar in the middle (fig. B, p. 59). As opposed to the first type of pointers, no secular objects resembling them in style and shape have been found in the vicinity. The influence of Persia is nevertheless evident, since one characteristically Persian type of pointer consists of a twisted four-sided bar, its tip shaped like a clenched fist with an outstretched index finger or like an open hand. Caucasian pointers of this type combine the Persian shape of the bar with a leaf-shaped tip of local origin. However, the latter element may likewise have originated in Persia, since the leaf design with wavy edges can also be found in one type of amulet from that region.[16]

Apart from serving to mark a passage when reciting the Torah, Caucasian pointers also had another distinctive use, recorded by Kasdai: "When the ark is opened, one of their respected congregants is given the honor of carrying the Torah scroll through the rows of worshipers . . . [and] when he comes to the *tevah* [reader's desk], he unrolls it slightly and displays the writing to those present on every side. The rabbi or *hakham* indicates with his pointer [*etzba*, literally "finger"] the beginning of the weekly portion, whereupon all of them declaim: 'And this is the law which Moses set before the children of Israel' . . ."[17]

It is possible that the phrase "To display the writing to the holy congregation," which recurs in some inscriptions engraved on Torah pointers such as the following: "This silver pointer was donated to display to the holy congregation of Israel the writing in a Torah scroll . . ." (Sc-474-77), alludes to a specific practice of the Mountain Jews, whereby one who raises the Torah simultaneously displays its lettering to the assembled worshipers. That conjecture is reinforced by a text found on several pointers: "This is the silver [pointer] with which one indicates [the writing of the Torah scroll] . . . [as] the Lord showed to Moses. . . ." The formula is evidently based on a midrashic interpretation of the verse (Numbers 8:4) that records God's instructions to Moses for constructing the seven-branched menorah: "Moses found it more perplexing to build the Menorah than to fashion any other implement in the Sanctuary – until the Almighty showed him how to do so with His finger" (Numbers Rabbah 15:3). The choice of this verse from Numbers and its interpretation in the midrash, which was no doubt familiar to members of the community, established a conceptual parallel between the guiding hand of the Lord and that of the *hakham* or reader during the Torah scroll's elevation.

The variety of names with which Mountain Jews referred to the pointer is wide and unusual, suggesting a range of traditions. Among the names also familiar in other Jewish communities, *etzba* (finger) and *kulmus* (quill) are most widely employed. It is an interesting fact that *etzba* is the Caucasian Jews' standard designation for the pointer, even though their pointers are not shaped like a finger or hand. These names are often combined with "[made] of silver," a reference to the material from which they are produced, and "silver article" or "silver plate" are other common terms. One Torah pointer is called *tzitz* (diadem or plate), a rare and exceptional designation for such an object (Sc-474-17). It presumably embodies that term's explanation in the Talmud, where the *tzitz* is said to have formed part of the High Priest's attire – "a kind of golden plate . . . on which 'Holy to the Lord' was written" (TB Sukkah 5a).

Some noteworthy inscriptions mention those days on which the Torah is read in synagogue. For example, one pointer from 1918 bears the following inscription: "This silver pointer (*etzba*) [which is intended] to display the writing of a Tor[ah] scroll to the holy congregation of Israel in the synagogue on Sabbaths, New Moons, Mondays and Thursdays and Festivals and High Holidays (?), was donated in exaltation of the soul of the youth Ya'akov, son of Binyamin, may he be granted eternal rest in the Garden of Eden, who perished in the city of Baku on Friday, the 28th day of Tishri 5679 [October 5, 1918]"

(Sc-474-84). This detailed formula sometimes appears in a cryptic version. Thus, when days on which the Torah is read are mentioned, their names appear as abbreviations rather than in full, e.g., "the days of *za-ha-v* [7-5-2, i.e., Saturday, Thursday, Monday] and *yo-t* [*yom tov*, i.e., festivals]" (Sc-474-42). On certain pointers the wording is extended to read "days of *za-ha-v* and *kesef*" (Sc-474-25), on others to "days of *za-ha-v, kesef,* and *nehoshet*" (Sc-474-54). In "days of *za-ha-v*" we have an obvious play on words, since *zahav* means "gold" in Hebrew. The expression, which initially referred to particular days of the week, acquired a meaning that transcended its original linguistic significance when *kesef* (silver) and *nehoshet* (copper) were attached to it. These three metals appear together in the list of materials from which vessels consecrated to God were fashioned (see Exodus 25:3, 31:4, etc.; Joshua 6:19); they are also listed together in the kabbalistic Book of Zohar.[18] Both there and in *Sha'arei Orah* (Gates of Light), a work by the medieval kabbalist Joseph Gikatila, they provide a mystical allusion to various qualities associated with three of the Ten Divine Emanations (*Sefirot*): "Gold, on the left, symbolizing the attribute of Power (*Din*); silver, on the right, symbolizing that of Love (*Hesed*); and copper symbolizing the attribute of Compassion (*Rahamim*)."

* * *

Woven cover for holy books, which belonged to the Abramov family of rabbis, Derbent, Dagestan, mid-19th century
Wool
H 47; W 30
Israel Museum Collection
Purchased with the help of Bruce Kovner, New York

The inscriptions engraved on Caucasian sacred objects in general also mirror historical or private events that had their impact on Jewish communal life. Thus, for example, the fifth group of finials (on which the names of Jacob's sons are inscribed) was produced during the first half of the twentieth century, when the Mountain Jews engaged in a widespread Zionist endeavor that transformed Caucasian Jewry into one national group. Choosing those particular names was an expression of the Zionist movement's aim to assemble the "Tribes of Israel" and reestablish Jewish sovereignty in Palestine. It may also have reflected the Caucasian Jews' traditional belief that they were descended from the "Lost Ten Tribes."

In the course of the Bolshevik Revolution and the Russian Civil War (1917–21), Jews were expelled from the Caucasus; many fled for their lives, others were butchered. Several dedicatory inscriptions mention the pogroms and hardships that members of the community had to endure. One example, engraved on a finial, pays tribute to three members of the same family – Miriam, daughter of Hayyim and her two children, Tzviyah and Nissim – who were murdered in 1918 (Sc-474-70). Similar formulas are also carved on tombstones.

Most of the Torah finials and pointers bear Hebrew inscriptions in square script of the Persian type, but some are engraved with semi-cursive ("Rashi") script. The lettering is often illegible and there are numerous spelling mistakes. From a few sample pointers we can trace the process of how an object was fashioned and how its inscription was engraved. In all likelihood it was purchased or ordered from a Muslim silversmith who designed the finial or pointer and saw to its ornamentation. In the course of his work he left a blank space for the inscription. Pointers had this space marked on the leaf-shaped tip that indicated the Torah reading. It is reasonable to assume that once the silversmith's work had been completed, certain items were handed over to a traditional scribe (*sofer stam*) or some other member of the community who was proficient in Hebrew lettering. One example shows that this pointer's engraving was not entrusted to a scribe, as it bears no inscription.

The notion that some inscriptions were engraved by expert scribes gains support from the clear and legible epigraphs that appear, for example, on a pair of finials (Sc-474-4) made in 1908 and dedicated in memory of Asher, son of Menasheh, as well as on a pointer (Sc-474-62) dating from 1914 and honoring the memory of Rahel, daughter of Shelomo. The scribe's expertise is demonstrated by his elegant lettering, the ruling (line adjustment), his ability to plan the space needed for the inscription, and the text's adjustment to that space. On a large number of items, however, the inscription is hard to decipher and someone unfamiliar with Hebrew lettering apparently engraved the text. In such cases it is reasonable to assume that the Muslim craftsman was given a Hebrew text of which he then made a garbled copy. It is nevertheless conceivable that some of these mistakes were due to the Caucasian Jews' limited knowledge of Hebrew, which resulted from the state campaign against Judaism. This was especially so during the Soviet regime, when use of the Hebrew alphabet was banned and Jewish cultural endeavor was inhibited to such an extent that most worshipers could no longer read Hebrew or follow the synagogue prayers. Even so, we have reason to believe that some of the Jews who wrote epigraphs on sacred objects or used them fully understood the meaning of those inscriptions and abbreviations. Thus, for example, a pair of finials from 1908 honoring the memory of Asher, son of Menasheh, have the *Anna be-Kho'ah* prayer engraved in a neat script and in its complete form, not merely the acrostic forty-two-letter Name of God derived from it. The engraver, presumably a traditional scribe, must have been familiar with this prayer and he chose to reproduce the full version.

1 This article is based on the documentation of sacred objects carried out by a team from the Hebrew University's Center for Jewish Art in conjunction with the Open University of St. Petersburg. The delegation that visited Azerbaijan and Dagestan in 1994 and 1997 comprised Dr. Aliza Cohen Mushlin, Valeri Dymshits, Boris Khaimovich, Grisha Manyuk, and Michael Kheifetz.

2 For demographic and historical changes within Caucasian Jewry, see the chapter on the history of the Mountain Jews, pp. 17–25.

3 The number in parentheses refers to the object's registration number in the Jerusalem index of the Center for Jewish Art.

4 The Divine Name of forty-two letters was evidently known as early as the first century CE. Its utilization is recorded in the Babylonian Talmud (Kiddushin 71a), but the text does not reveal its constituent letters. In his commentary on the Talmud (Kiddushin, loc. cit.; Sanhedrin, 101b, 60a), Rashi declares that the Name is hidden and unknown.

5 The traveler Joseph Chorny, who visited Kuba in 1868, claimed to have seen there a *keter Torah* (Torah crown, a term probably used to denote finals; see p. 56) with an inscription dated 1761 (see Altshuler, *Jews of the Eastern Caucasus*, p. 207).

6 This item is now in the Cymbalista collection, Tel Aviv.

7 On Judeo-Tat and its relationship with Iranian dialects, see above, p. 37. On the relation between the names of neighborhoods and synagogues and the names of places of origin of the community, see the chapter about Caucasian Jewish construction, pp. 65 ff.

8 Yaniv, *Content and Form*, pp. 96–129, indicates that the term *keter* (Hebrew for "crown") stems from this object's development from the Torah crown surmounting a Persian Torah case. There is a structural resemblance between the type of finial known as *keter* and the crest surmounting the local form of Torah case, but it should be emphasized that this term is also applied to very differently shaped finials whose relationship with the crest, in regard to structure and development, is questionable. It is my considered opinion that one should ascribe this term as used by the Mountain Jews not to the object's historical evolution but to the term's origin in the Persian area.

9 As an honorific term, *keter* has well-known applications in other contexts. Several examples may be quoted, e.g. "Three are crowned with old age and length of days" (Genesis Rabbah 59:6) and "He praises [literally, 'weaves crowns for'] his Creator" (TB Hagigah 13b).

10 Evidence regarding the use of Torah cases may be found in a traveler's account of his visit to the Caucasus in 1887: "Their Torah scrolls are fitted into wooden cases that open ... from top to bottom" (Kasdai, *The Kingdom of Ararat*, p. 48). Ever since Jews from Russia settled in the Caucasus, a merger of customs has been evident in the synagogues of that region: alongside Torah scrolls housed in cases, bearing witness to the original practice, there are now scrolls dressed in mantles which point to the influence of Ashkenazi tradition. In two Eastern Jewish communities, those of Cochin and Aden, there was a custom of setting a crown over the Torah case. The team of the Center for Jewish Art documented one fragment of a Torah crown which, on the evidence of its structure, must be related to the East-European Ashkenazi tradition.

11 In The Jewish Museum, New York, there is a collection of finials which resemble those of the Caucasus in their spherical shape, divided in half by an encircling band, and in some of the inscriptions engraved on them. According to information supplied in the catalogue documenting the collection (Grafman, *Crowning Glory*), these finials were made in twentieth-century Persia and all of them were donated by Dr. Harry G. Friedman. I have no knowledge of early Persian finials of this type and believe that these examples should be studied so as to ascertain their visual origin.

12 For a comparison, see Hanegbi and Yaniv, *Afghanistan*, pp. 92–110.

13 Arbel and Magal, *In the Land of the Golden Fleece*, pp. 158–60.

14 For a comparison of the shape and inscriptions, see (for example) Arbel and Magal, loc. cit.

15 See also Hanegbi and Yaniv (above, n. 12), pp. 92–93, fig. no. 2. On p. 89 of *Sefer Segulot* (The Book of Remedies, 1867), a work written in Kuba now in the Gross Family Collection, Tel Aviv, these forty-two letters are mentioned as part of the formula to be written on an amulet.

16 Shrire, *Hebrew Amulets*, pp. 143–70 (plates 5, 14, 28).

17 Kasdai (above, n. 10), loc.cit.

18 Zohar II (Exodus), Terumah, 148a, and Va-Yak'hel, 197b; Zohar I (Genesis), omitted passages, 267a.

The Characteristic Features of Caucasian Jewish Construction

Boris Khaimovich

In the second half of the nineteenth century, there was a Jewish population in about forty settlements in Azerbaijan and Dagestan. According to data from the 1886 census, there were large concentrations of Jews in Kuba (6,282), Derbent (1,671), Vartashen, renamed Oguz (1,396), Majalis (529), and Temir-Khan-Shura, renamed Buinaksk (334).[1]

Jewish communities began to form in these towns and villages in the late eighteenth–early nineteenth centuries as a result of the compulsory transfer of entire communities from one district to another, and, soon afterwards, of the voluntary migration of individual families who desired to live in a Jewish environment. The differences between the communities in terms of the style of construction of their homes, synagogues, and even tombstones reflect differences in environmental influences and in the conditions of their life.

The Jewish Quarter

Kuba

The Jewish Quarter of the city of Kuba was a town in its own right. Established in the late seventeenth century, it was populated exclusively by Jews and was even named the Jewish Quarter (Yevreiskaya Sloboda);[2] after the Revolution, its name was changed to the Red Quarter (Krasnaya Sloboda). Its first inhabitants migrated from villages in the Caspian Sea coast between Kuba and Derbent, and also from villages in the highlands. Its neighborhoods were named after the names of the villages from which their residents originated: Karchagi, Kusari, Kulkati, Chapkeni.[3] In the late eighteenth century, Jews who had been transferred to Kuba from the Gilan region in Persia established the Gilaki neighborhood. Other Persian Jews founded the Agadgeni neighborhood. The population of the Quarter underwent its major growth in the first half of the nineteenth century. The Karui neighborhood, whose name features on the dedicatory inscription of the synagogue (see ill. on p. 69), was established in the same period, probably by Jews from a village in the Dgigut Katta valley in the Kiyurin district.[4] The Eastern neighborhood, the last to be established, was populated by local residents who had moved from the upper to the lower (wealthier) parts of the Quarter. Each neighborhood had its own synagogue and its own section in the cemetery.

All the neighborhoods faced the Quarter's main street, which ran parallel to the river. Residents recall that the houses were crowded together rather than built according to an orderly street plan. Remains of the original construction are still visible in the poorer areas of the Quarter, situated on the hill. Most of the older houses were built in the late nineteenth century from flat bricks and had red-tiled roofs. The most popular builder in the late nineteenth and early twentieth century was Hillel Ben-Hayyim, who constructed many brick houses and synagogues in a unique, richly ornamented style. Most of the houses were two stories high. The ground floor of the houses that faced the main street often contained small shops or workshops, many belonging to shoemakers. The open or closed balconies

Opposite:
The Jewish Quarter (Krasnaya Sloboda) seen from the Jewish cemetery, Kuba, Azerbaijan
Photo taken in 1994

on the second floor bestowed a colorful appearance on the street. Wealthy families in this period embellished their houses with a wide range of ornamentation – stone and wood carvings, square pillars, caryatids (pillars shaped like female figures topped by a flat capital) – in a Russian colonial style, which probably came to Kuba from the city of Baku. Most houses had closed courtyards, which were used during the festival of Sukkot. The *sukkah* (booth in which Jews traditionally dwell during the seven days of the festival) was erected from *palas* rugs, and its roof was covered with branches.

A wave of new construction has recently swept over Krasnaya Sloboda. Many old houses were razed or totally renovated, and the Quarter has taken on a new appearance. Nonetheless, many of the modern houses preserve the style of the 1920s. Carved wood panels decorate the houses of wealthier residents, such as that located near the Kusari synagogue, whose facade is adorned with a wood carving of a flower in a vase.

Vartashen (Oguz)

The Jewish Quarter of Vartashen was established in the late seventeenth century, when the Khan of Shemakha settled sixty Jewish families from the Gilan region in Persia in the lower part of this hilly area. About half of the population at the time was Christian (Armenians and Udins), and the

A house in the Jewish Quarter of Kuba, Azerbaijan
Photo taken in 1994

other half was Muslim. In the 1860s, a total of 190 Jewish families lived in Vartashen. Following a conflict in the late 1980s, the Azerbaijanis expelled the Armenians from Vartashen and changed the name of the village to Oguz.

Beginning in the late nineteenth century, the Jews of Vartashen constructed large buildings using a combination of unworked fieldstones and rows of flat bricks. Previously, as was the practice in the Caucasus, unbaked bricks were used, but they required constant plastering.[5] The typical interior plan of houses in the region consisted of a pen for horses and cows on the ground floor and three rooms on the upper floor – one for the men, a second for the women and children, and a third for guests. The houses stood within courtyards encompassed by a high stone wall that faced the street on one side. Many of the Jewish houses boasted large stone gates with carved wooden doors surmounted by an awning. A plaque bearing the name of the builder and construction date was often affixed next to the gate. Particularly striking was the entrance to the house of the Yousufov family, built, according to a member of the family, some 150 years ago, whose wall was adorned with two carved lions reminiscent of those found in Persian drawings. Conical clay ovens used for baking bread are preserved in many courtyards in the Jewish Quarter of Vartashen.

A house in the Jewish Quarter of Vartashen (Oguz), Azerbaijan
Photo taken in 1999

The synagogue of the Karui
(Karchagi) community,
Kuba, Azerbaijan
Photo taken in 1994

Majalis

Majalis is a large village to the north of Dagestan that was inhabited by Jews and Muslims (Dargins and Qumiqs). While the Jewish Quarter in Majalis, as in Vartashen, was situated in the lower, wealthier part of the village, most of its houses were considerably more modest, built of straw and clay bricks and only one story high.

Derbent

In the late eighteenth century, the Khan of Kazikomokh destroyed the village of Abusubo, which had a large Jewish population. These Jews moved to Derbent, and their numbers increased following the Russian conquest of the city in 1813. Unlike the Jews of Kuba, who lived in a well-defined quarter, Derbent's Jewish residents were dispersed throughout the lower part of the city, which was built according to a master plan. The buildings, most of which were constructed in the second half of the nineteenth century, were built in a neoclassical style, as in other cities of southern Russia. The houses of Jews, like those of non-Jews, lay within courtyards bounded by high walls. The facades of the houses and walls were ornamented, as was customary in the area, with flat columns, inlaid stones, and cornices that ran along the roof.

Buinaksk

Founded in 1863 as a border fortress named Temir-Khan-Shura, the city contained a Jewish population whose members came from the nearby villages and, as in Derbent, were scattered throughout the settlement. In the second half of the nineteenth century a relatively large community of Ashkenazi Jews developed in Buinaksk.[6]

Synagogues (*Nimaz*)

In the early twentieth century, there were forty-four synagogues in Azerbaijan and Dagestan.[7] The largest concentration was in Kuba, which, according to the accounts of residents, contained eleven synagogues. By 1996, the total number of synagogues had dwindled to five.[8]

Kuba

Gilah, the central synagogue of Kuba, is active to the present day (see ill. on p. 71). It was established in 1896 by Jews from the Gilan region in Persia, as testified in a plaque set in the wall next to the gate, and bears the name of its builder, Hillel Ben-Hayyim, on its facade. An additional plaque, apparently transferred from an earlier building and now set in the entrance, refers to the year 1857.[9] The characteristic

Memorial inscription engraved in stone on the wall of the synagogue of the Karui (Karchagi) community, Kuba, Azerbaijan, 1816
Photo taken in 1994

feature of the Gilah synagogue is its slanting roof, over which lies an octagonal drum surmounted by a dome. There are four windows in each of the structure's three walls, totaling twelve for the twelve tribes of Israel (the windows of the nineteenth-century synagogue in Nalchik, in southern Russia, are arranged in a similar fashion).[10] The prayer hall measures seventeen by seventeen meters. In the center of its ceiling is a square inner cupola covered by an octagonal outer drum with windows that were once glazed, enabling natural light to penetrate the synagogue from above. The design of the Gilah synagogue may have been influenced by a mosque with a similar roof built in the city in the second half of the nineteenth century.

The Torah ark is set in a niche in the wall, closed by four doors and surrounded by a stucco relief of foliate ornamentation and birds. Next to it is the octagonal *bimah* (reader's platform), with a heavy desk (*tevah*) on which the Torah scroll is placed. Rugs cover the floor of the synagogue; it was

The new synagogue in
Vartashen (Oguz),
Azerbaijan
Photo taken in 1994

customary for congregants to leave their shoes in the vestibule and enter the prayer hall barefooted. Some recall that in the distant past there was a water fountain for washing hands and feet.[11] Initially, worshipers sat on the floor, but now benches fill the hall and line its walls.[12] In the past there was no women's section, and on holidays women gathered in the synagogue courtyard and followed the service from there. Today, they are permitted to enter the vestibule.

Hillel Ben-Hayyim also built a synagogue for the Karui community (see ills. on pp. 68 and 69), which, according to the dedicatory inscription, was inaugurated in 1906. An additional plaque, transferred from an earlier site, bears the date 1816. As in the Gilah synagogue, the slanting roof is surmounted by an octagonal drum with a cupola. This synagogue is distinguished by its windows, which are diversely shaped and placed at different heights. They originally held colored glass that created multicolored light patterns in the prayer hall. The prayer hall was surmounted by an eight-petal dome reminiscent of the concealed domes of wooden synagogues in Poland. The influence of Eastern European (Ashkenazi) Jewry in the Caucasus was also evident in the Great Synagogue of Derbent (no longer extant), which exhibited similar features.[13] Traces of drawings of foliate motifs and blue jars on a red background are visible in the inner dome and in the wooden frame around the Torah ark.

The Kusari synagogue (see ills. on pp. 74 and 75) is the most prominent structure in the Jewish Quarter of Kuba. Built in the early twentieth century, it stands on a small hill next to the riverbank and soars to a height of fourteen meters. Its dimensions (fourteen by twenty-two meters) are also outstanding. A decorative tower rises from each of the four corners of the slanting roof, the top of which is adorned with two tent-shaped towers, which give the Quarter its distinctive skyline. The building is framed by a row of large, round windows, each pair of which is set within a pointed arch. The narthex on the eastern side is adorned with large, raised jars. The Torah ark (6.3 meters high and 2.62 meters wide) conforms to the dimensions of the large hall, and its nine compartments are each fitted with its own door.

In the early twentieth century, Hillel Ben-Hayyim also built the Rabba synagogue on the main street of the Jewish Quarter of Kuba. Its octagonal dome was not preserved. The building was used as a carpet shop and workshop after the synagogue ceased to function in the 1970s.

Derbent

An 1842 map of Derbent shows only one synagogue, adjacent to the city's southern wall. In the mid-nineteenth century there were three synagogues, and the total rose to eleven by the early

Platform with *tevah* and Torah ark in the Gilah synagogue of Kuba, Azerbaijan
Photo taken in 1944

Torah ark, platform, and
tevah in the Derbent
synagogue, Dagestan
Photo taken in 1994

twentieth century. By 1994, the city was once again left with a single synagogue. According to an inscription on one of its walls, it was restored after a fire in 1914 thanks to a donation by someone named Hanukayev. A wall of the Dadayev synagogue has also been preserved. The two structures were built of local stone in the classical colonial style and stood in a row with the nearby houses, in contrast to the usual practice of building synagogues within courtyards.

The vestibule of the Hanukayev synagogue contains a small prayer hall for weekday use. The main prayer hall is built breadthwise, unlike those in Kuba, and its exceptional shape may result not only from the constraints of the land on which it lies but also from local tradition; indeed, two similar synagogues are found in Vartashen. Another distinctive feature of the Hanukayev synagogue is a four-column construction encompassing the *bimah* in the center of the hall and containing a drum with windows that provide the main source of illumination (see ill. above). A similar construction is characteristic of many synagogues in Turkey and Western Georgia.

The Torah ark is framed by two round pillars topped by lotus-shaped capitals and colored in a rich array of green, purple, violet, and gold on an azure background. The top of the Torah ark features the names of the three Patriarchs. The floor of the prayer hall is covered with rugs on which chairs are arranged in rows. A ritual slaughterhouse is located next to the synagogue.

Vartashen (Oguz)

Two synagogues are preserved in the Jewish Quarter of Vartashen. The old synagogue was built in 1849 within a closed courtyard. In 1994, the community restored the building, and it resumed its function as a synagogue. Distinguished by its breadthwise construction (thirteen by twenty-two meters), the synagogue comprises a prayer hall divided by a row of columns into two sections of equal size and a women's section on the second floor, added in the recent renovation. There are three entrances along the lengthwise wall of the structure. The surrounding square courtyard bears a great resemblance to those of the local mosques.

The second synagogue (see ill. on p. 70) was built in the early twentieth century in a small square in the center of the Jewish Quarter. Like most of the buildings in the village, it was constructed of a combination of unchiseled stones and inlaid rows of bricks. Its southern wall, the most striking, had three portals, two of which are now sealed. The main facade is adorned by rusticated pilasters in the corners and a curved cornice. Its inner space is undivided, and the prayer hall, measuring nine by eighteen meters, contains a relatively shallow (fifty-centimeter) Torah ark niche, which is surrounded by decorative bricks.

According to local inhabitants, the house next to the synagogue was the rabbi's residence, and also served for sessions of the rabbinical court and for the ritual slaughtering of meat.

Buinaksk

Built in 1862, the synagogue of Buinaksk has been preserved to the present day. The large (nineteen by sixteen meters) red-brick structure was built in the neo-Renaissance style. Its distinction in the region lies in its combination of Caucasian and Ashkenazi Jewish traditions. The women's section, situated along the northern wall, was part of the building's original plan. Its construction is longitudinal, on a north-south axis. The Torah ark, like its Eastern European counterparts, is elevated, with access provided by a number of steps, but the use of the platform as a *bimah* sets it apart from Ashkenazi tradition. The ceiling and walls are covered with plaster reliefs and paintings that create the illusion of curtains. Round stucco medallions surround the hooks in the ceiling from which five chandeliers are suspended.

This was the first synagogue in the Caucasus in which benches were installed, and evidence to the controversy that surrounded their introduction in the late nineteenth century is recorded in the writings of the traveler Kasdai: "They made themselves both [freestanding] benches and wall benches, even though there were still pious men among them, especially from the older generation, who did not wish to sit on benches. They sat on the floor in their stockinged feet and stared with disdain and repulsion at the heretics who introduced the benches into the synagogue and sat on them during the prayers."[14]

Torah ark of the Kusari
synagogue, Kuba, Azerbaijan
Photo taken in 1994

Cemeteries

In the settlements in which there remains a Jewish community (Kuba, Derbent, Vartashen, and Buinaksk), cemeteries are well maintained. Most of the tombstones in the Majalis cemetery have been destroyed, and the cemetery has fallen into disrepair. In other settlements (Gianja, Ismailli, Karchagi, Mingchaur, Shaki, Shemakha), tombstones have been preserved in fairly good condition even though no substantial Jewish community remains. With no one to maintain these cemeteries, however, their fate is uncertain.

In Kuba, Vartashen, and Majalis, where Jewish inhabitants resided together in quarters, the Jewish cemeteries were situated on the adjacent hills. The tombstones in these cemeteries greatly resemble one another in shape, in the direction they face (westward), and in the content and style of their inscriptions.

The relatively narrow and thin tombstones, placed on the ground at the head of the grave, are reminiscent of Muslim tombstones. Only the older stones of Vartashen, preserved in the old part of the Vartashen cemetery, on the green slope of the hill, differ in style: they consist of elongated blocks of minimally worked fieldstone. Though a few Hebrew letters are visible on the tombstones, most of the

inscriptions and dates are too worn to be decipherable. Similar stones that have sunk into the earth over the course of time can also be seen in remote sections of the Kuba cemetery. Stones with shapes resembling those in Vartashen and Kuba were discovered in the village of Shudukh, at a location identified by local residents as the former Jewish cemetery. Pre-nineteenth-century tombstones, which have become lost in the rocky terrain into which they settled over time, may also have been made of carved fieldstones.[15]

The earliest tombestones, from 1807 and 1814, were discovered in the Kuba cemetery.[16] Carved from fieldstone, they were about eighty centimeters high, with the inscription chiseled into the facade of the stone slab. Other tombstones from the first half of the nineteenth century are rectangular stela, about one meter high, and free of ornamentation. Modest decoration appears on mid-nineteenth-century tombstones in the form of an open rosette, and those from the second half of the nineteenth century are decorated with leaves and Star-of-David motifs. Inscriptions are framed in a pointed arch. The tombstones in Derbent (the earliest of which dates from 1847), Karchagi (the earliest of which dates from 1851), and Majalis are of similar shape. A singular characteristic of the tombstones in Majalis is the double arch of the Tablets of the Law, which contain the initial letters of the beginning of the epitaph.

The Kusari synagogue in Kuba, Azerbaijan
Photo taken in 2000

Tombstones in the Jewish
cemetery of Majalis,
Dagestan
Photo taken in 1994

Towards the late nineteenth century, a new type of tombstone began to appear in Caucasian Jewish cemeteries in the form of sarcophagi and mausoleums. In Kuba, they were built of a single stone, raised on a number of steps and covered by a kind of awning. In Majalis, they were constructed of bricks in the shape of a flat-roofed house with an adjoining traditional tombstone.[17] The greatest range of tombstones and carved decorations is found in the cemeteries of Buinaksk, a town in which many Ashkenazi Jews resided. Late nineteenth- and early twentieth-century tombstones are adorned with both traditional Ashkenazi elements (the Star of David, the Tablets of the Law, the Priestly Blessing) and typical Islamic geometrical decorations such as the crescent moon. The presence of Islamic elements may be explained not only by the influence of the surrounding population but also by the fact that the stonecutters who made the tombstones were Muslims.

The inscriptions engraved on tombstones from the nineteenth century were uniform and concise, carved in square letters. The longer ones contain descriptions such as "an upright man," "a distinguished person," or even: "A pursuer of justice and mercy has been cut down."[18] Tombstones also indicate the exact date of death, including the year, month, day of the month, and day of the week. The cause of death is sometimes mentioned as well, as in this 1859 inscription from the Kuba cemetery: "[slayed] at the hands of a cruel Gentile."[19] The acronym of the phrase "May his soul be bound up in the bond of eternal life" is rarely found inscribed on older tombstones, but quite common on many tombstones from the late nineteenth century belonging to Ashkenazi families. In that period it became common to note the year of birth and death on the tombstone in an abbreviated form. In the early twentieth century, Russian texts began to appear in addition to the Hebrew inscriptions on tombstones.

1   These figures are taken from charts published by Anisimov in the article "Mountain Jews," pp. 161–332.
2   *Collection* (Tiflis), pp. 19–44. In 1996, only fifteen non-Jews resided in the Quarter, amidst 5, 500 Jews.
3   See Miller, *Tats*, p. 25.
4   Ibid., p. 28.
5   See Bezhanov, "Vartashen," pp. 113–14.
6   See Altshuler, *Jews of the Eastern Caucasus*, p. 344.
7   Ibid., p. 343.
8   The information about synagogues is based on material collected by two joint research expeditions of the Hebrew University's Center for Jewish Art and the Jewish University in St. Petersburg in 1994 and 1996.
9   During the eighteenth and nineteenth centuries, synagogues were first built as temporary structures; only after the tolerance of their neighbors had been established did the Jews erect a permanent building. This may account for the fact that in some synagogues there are two plaques – one bearing the date of construction, and the other, apparently transferred from an older site, bearing an earlier date.
10 Chorny, *Book of Travels*, p. 21.
11 Ibid.
12 See Altshuler (above, no. 6), p. 347.
13 Chorny (above, no. 10), p. 5.
14 Kasdai, "Travel Letters," p. 113.
15 Babalikashvili, *Jewish Inscriptions*, pp. 112–140.
16 Fifty-three tombstones, two of which bear the remarkably early dates of 1684/5 and 1692, were discovered in the ancient village of Abusubo. See Yishai, "Jewish Settlement," pp. 94–95.
17 Tombstones somewhat similar to these, shaped like a flat-roofed house, were found in the small town of Ahaltzich in Western Georgia.
18 It should be noted that no graves of women from the nineteenth century have been discovered.
19 Babalikashvili (above, no. 15), p. 132.

Tombstone in the Jewish cemetery of Kuba, Azerbaijan
Photo taken in 1994

The Cycle of the Year
Liya Mikdash-Shamailov

Until the first half of the nineteenth century, the Caucasian Jewish community preserved a number of ancient traditions that had apparently survived as a result of its prolonged isolation from other Jewish communities.[1] Following pogroms in Kuba (1741–44), the community was bereft of rabbinical leadership, and religious life was revived by five rabbis called in from Berdichev in the Ukraine. It seems, however, that a much more significant process of exposure to the Jewish world outside occurred in the mid-nineteenth century, when Caucasian Jewish merchants began attending trade fairs and establishing commercial ties with Jewish merchants from Turkey, Persia, Poland, Lithuania, and Russia.[2] These encounters led to the adoption of practices followed in other communities and, as a result, to the gradual disappearance of many of their own ancient traditions. This chapter deals only with customs peculiar to the Caucasian Jewish community.

The Sabbath

Although the father (*bebe*) was, from time immemorial, the absolute ruler of the extended family (*kele-kiflet*), on Fridays his authority was assumed by the mother (*dedey*) or grandmother (*kele-dedey*), who then reigned supreme over the household. In honor of the Sabbath, several families – either relatives or neighbors – gathered to slaughter cattle or poultry and the housewife then koshered the meat. Fresh bread was baked every Friday, and the streets would fill with women carrying trays on their heads and bundles of twigs in their hands to heat the oven. The oven served either to heat or to cook food for the Sabbath, and a Muslim *Shabbes goy* was charged with the task of stoking it on the Sabbath day.

As the Sabbath drew near, people were called upon to assist communal officials: before the beginning of the Sabbath, the *shammash* (beadle in Hebrew) of the synagogue (*goboy-nimaz*) went from house to house collecting money, bread, eggs, and so on from the women. Housewives also dispatched Sabbath food to needy families.

While the men gathered in the synagogue, youngsters walked along the streets carrying plates of food covered with clean cloths that were exchanged with relatives of the family. This practice enabled each family to set a rich and varied Sabbath table. One essential dish was *yepreghi* (or *yepereghi*), cabbage stuffed with meat and rice and boiled in chicken soup. Before being served, it was doused in a sauce made from *elu*, a sour local fruit. Another item was *osh*, a rice stew demanding skillful preparation as the grains of rice could not be allowed to stick together. After the end of the Sabbath, women prepared *xingala-yngar*, squares of dough made of flour, garlic, and wine vinegar that were cooked in a rich meat soup. On the Sabbath it was customary to visit the homes of older men and scholars to hear them expound the Torah.

Today, the Sabbath is still kept and every effort is made to be present at the family's Sabbath table. However, some key features of Sabbath observance – such as attending synagogue – have vanished.

Opposite:
Reading the *haggadah* on the night of Passover, Kuba, Azerbaijan, late 19th century
Photo courtesy of Beth Hatefutsoth, The Nahum Goldmann Museum of the Jewish Diaspora, Tel Aviv

Sabbath candlesticks,
Azerbaijan, 20th century
Brass, silver, Bakelite
Israel Museum Collection,
purchased with the help of
Bruce Kovner, New York
Lent by the Haifa Museum
of Ethnology
Lent by Taylo Mardekhayev,
Nahariya

Rosh ha-Shanah

Evidence from the first half of the nineteenth century reveals that this festival, which occurs on the first day of the Hebrew month of Tishri (corresponding roughly to September-October), did not mark the beginning of the New Year for Caucasian Jews. At that time they still regarded the New Moon of the month of Nisan (April) as the beginning of the year. On the first day of Tishri it was customary to read from the Torah and to sound the *shofar* in accordance with the biblical precept: "In the seventh month, on the first day of the month, you shall have a sacred convocation: you may perform no creative work; it is a day of blowing the horn for you" (Numbers 29:1). Caucasian

Jews abstained from work on this festival and held it to be a day of rejoicing. Girls dressed in fine clothes walked about in groups to the accompaniment of songs and drums.

By the second half of the nineteenth century, the first day of Tishri had been acknowledged as Rosh ha-Shanah and a two-day festival was celebrated. On the eve of Rosh ha-Shanah (and not, as with other Jewish communities, on the eve of Yom Kippur), the head of the family and firstborn sons (*xelef-bexuri*) performed the *kapparot* ritual (*nedovo*, meaning "atonement").[3] Performing this ritual on the eve of Rosh ha-Shanah has been maintained in Azerbaijan down to our own time. After the festive meal, prayers were recited and half of the Book of Psalms was read; the entire Book of Psalms was read twice in the morning and passages from the Mishnah in the evening. It was customary not to sleep throughout both days of the festival, since God was thought to be judging men's deeds at that time. On the second night, prayers were recited close to the river and it was customary to fast a day before and a day after Rosh ha-Shanah. Lamb's head soup, pumpkin dishes, fish, dates, honey, carrots, and apples were traditional holiday fare.

Customs associated with the festival underwent a further change during the latter part of the twentieth century. People now observe the *tashlikh* ceremony (reciting prayers near a source of water in order to "cast" their sins into the water), which is linked with an old Caucasian Jewish practice: ridding oneself of bad dreams by "telling them to the river."

Yom Kippur (*Ruz Kipur*)

According to evidence from the second half of the nineteenth century, Yom Kippur was a fast day that also applied to animals.

Until the second half of the twentieth century, the *kapparot* ritual was performed not on the eve of Yom Kippur but on the day before Rosh ha-Shanah, as mentioned above. In accordance with local

Box and pouch for fragrant leaves and spices; candlesticks; and candle used for *havdalah* (the ceremony that marks the end of the Sabbath), 20th century
Brass, tin, silk, wax
Candle: L 46
Candlesticks: H 5.5
Lent by the Haifa Museum of Ethnology
Lent by Frieda Yosifov, Acre

custom, one light was kindled in synagogue for the entire community on Yom Kippur eve. The playing of a flute, not the sounding of a shofar, announced the end of Yom Kippur. On leaving the synagogue, worshipers kissed the rabbi's hands while young people kissed the hands of older men and asked for forgiveness. That night, every Jew stepped out to the courtyard of his house with the wine over which blessing is said on the Sabbath and holidays, and marked with a stick the location where he would build the wooden hut (*sukkah*) in which the family would dwell during the festival of Sukkot.

In recent times, it has become common to perform the *kapparot* ritual on Yom Kippur eve as well as on the eve of Rosh ha-Shanah. On the day before Yom Kippur (*me'alumei mi'id*), women bake bread while men and youngsters bring live fowls to the rabbi sitting in the synagogue. A cockerel is slaughtered for every male child as well as for the unborn child of an expectant mother, and a hen is slaughtered for every female child. Fresh bread and the *kapparah* chickens are then allotted to needy members of the community.

On the eve of Yom Kippur, when lights are kindled in the home for each member of the family, they are placed on two trays – one for the living and another in memory of the departed. An additional light is kindled for pregnant women. The lights are inserted in damp soil to remind people of the place they are bound for when they die. After the lights are kindled, all members of the family proceed to the synagogue. Women do not go inside but gather in the courtyard and listen to the service through the windows. On the day of Yom Kippur, it is customary to visit friends, kiss the hands of older men, and ask for forgiveness. Traditionally, special importance is attached to visiting families that have lost one of their members during the past year. The end of Yom Kippur is now signaled by the rabbi blowing the shofar.

Sukkot (*Suko, Aravo*)

The festival was called *aravo* (after *arava*, the Hebrew word for "willow"), since Caucasian Jews believed that the ritual connected with willow branches on the seventh day of the festival, Hoshana Rabbah (see next page), was the essential feature of Sukkot. During the first half of the nineteenth century, people did not celebrate Simhat Torah (the Rejoicing of the Law), and of the Four Species (citron, palm branch, myrtle, and willow) only the willows were known. On the eve of the festival it was customary for families to begin "dwelling" in their *sukkah*. On the eighth day, they brought a portion of their crops to a "religious place," in keeping with the description of Sukkot as a harvest festival (Exodus 23:16).[4] It was customary to read from the Torah, sing, and climb to the rooftops with jugs of water which were poured over the walls of the houses as greetings were exchanged with friends and insults were hurled at enemies. No special name was given to this custom, which may be linked with Simhat Beit ha-Sho'evah, the ancient Water-Drawing Celebration.

Asking for forgiveness on Yom Kippur (the Day of Atonement), Kuba, Azerbaijan, 2000

By the mid-nineteenth century, the practice of taking all of the Four Species had been adopted. On the eve of the festival, synagogue services were prolonged and, after a meal in the *sukkah*, prayers were recited for another three hours. Families dwelled in their *sukkah* throughout the festival and each morning a blessing was recited over the Four Species.

On 21 of Tishri, the eve of Hoshana Rabbah, it was customary to honor the memory of those who had died without offspring. Worshipers kindled a light in the synagogue and placed it before the rabbi; each in turn recited verses from the last chapter of the Torah and the whole of Psalms. They observed a night-long vigil in the synagogue, because of the tradition that man's sentence is finally pronounced on the night of Hoshana Rabbah. The next morning people underwent a ritual cleansing from sin which, in other communities, was performed on the eve of Yom Kippur. The rabbi gave each worshiper forty strokes on the back, using a whip of thongs made from an ass's hide, and was handed silver coins in return. That same morning the *shammash* would bring heaps of willow or poplar branches to the synagogue for the customary beating of the willows. Each man took a bundle of twigs for himself and another for someone who was absent, pointed them upwards, and beat them on the floor. Congregants bearing Torah scrolls then made seven circuits (*hakkafot* in Hebrew) around the platform (*bimah*), on which the scrolls were placed when the circuits had been completed. Male worshipers gathered in the synagogue and recited chapters of the Psalms. When they emerged from the synagogue, young boys and girls waiting outside burst into song and dance. Rabbis watched the dancers, but refrained from joining their circle as doing so would be deemed undignified. After the service the willow branches were brought home and hung by the entrance. They remained there until the following year, or until Passover, when they were sometimes used for the traditional search for bread crumbs preceding the festival.

Two particular customs were observed on that day. The first, no longer extant, consisted in members of the community pouring water over each other; the second, *nedovo gürda* (the Celebration of Vows Fulfilled), still survives (among older people at least), and relates to vows made and kept during the past year. A sheep or cockerel is usually slaughtered and money, bread, or clothing distributed to members of the community. One special custom that all the Mountain Jews follow to this day is preparing a meal before sunrise on the morning of Hoshana Rabbah. This meal includes a barley gruel (*ghurghuti*) and meat balls, and every effort is made to consume it before daybreak. In the morning, parents distribute nuts to their children for the "nut game" (*qerebech vozi*), in which a hole 20-25 centimeters wide is dug in the ground and children then try to throw nuts in it.

The following day, Simhat Torah (*ruz aravo*), marks the high point of the festival, and on the eve of the holiday joyous festivities take place in synagogue. A procession, headed by the rabbis and other dignitaries carrying Torah scrolls, makes seven circuits around the platform. Men hold lighted

Lighting candles on Yom Kippur eve, Kuba, Azerbaijan, 2000

candles and sing traditional songs. At an "auction" held before the festival, the honor of carrying a scroll is purchased by the highest bidder.

In recent years, partly as a result of anti-religious propaganda on the part of the (former) Communist regime, the number of Jews still maintaining these holiday traditions has dwindled. Most people no longer build a kosher *sukkah* of their own, using instead any existing structure in their courtyard, but synagogues continue to build a communal *sukkah*. Whereas most men congregate in this *sukkah* on the eve of the festival, only few do so during the seven days of the festival.

Hanukkah

A description of Caucasian Jewish practices dating from 1837 makes no mention of the festival of Hanukkah. Indeed, no Hanukkah lamps from synagogues or private homes are to be found. Around the mid-nineteenth century, however, people began to kindle Hanukkah lights, attaching them with a lump of earth to the inner wall of the house, next to the *mezuzah* at the entrance. This practice blackened the wall with soot, which had to be covered with whitewash after the eight-day festival. Accordingly, in recent years it has become customary to place the lights on a tray by the door, on a window sill, or on a balcony. Up to the Second World War, all Jewish males learned Hebrew and could recite the prayers, and it was they who kindled the Hanukkah lights. Recently, it has become accepted for women to kindle the lights even though they cannot recite the prayers. A Hanukkah

Slaughtering poultry for
Rosh ha-Shanah, Kuba,
Azerbaijan, 2000

rice pudding (*osh ḥanukoy*), as well as a pilaf of rice, squash, and dried fruits, are served on the first night of the holiday. Much the same custom prevails among the Jews of Sene (Kurdistan), who eat the last of the season's squash on Hanukkah. Children born during the festival are usually named Hanukkah or Nissim.

Tu bi-Shevat (*Shev Idor*)

This festival's local name, *Shev Idor*, means "Evening of the Trees." The strong link that Caucasian Jews bore to the land and agriculture in general aroused tense expectation as the holiday approached, because of a tradition according to which the fate of trees – which would or would not bear fruit – was determined on this day. The poplar was compared to a childless family: just as that family yearns for a child, so the barren tree longs to be fruitful. Legend has it that on Tu bi-Shevat eve the poplar and the willow shed tears when they learn that they are doomed to remain barren in the coming year; other trees laugh and rejoice. To emphasize the grain's importance, a dish of fried wheat (*ghare-ghoru*) combined with nuts and raisins is prepared in the evening. A pilaf comprising mainly of dried fruit is also served, while dried fruits (*xushke er-emish*) produced during the last twelve months adorn the festive table.

Purim (*Homunu*)

On Ta'anit Esther, the day before the festival of Purim, each housewife prepares holiday food to await her husband's return from the synagogue. These dishes include halvah (*ḥasido*, a confection based on crushed nuts and honey or sugar), flour fried in butter, and *lavash* – a very thin kind of pita. In the evening, *mishloah manot* (food gifts), chiefly comprising of *lavash* and halvah, are given to the poor. Studies from the late nineteenth century record a Purim custom that was observed in the Vartashen region of Azerbaijan: children made a wooden effigy of Haman, and on Purim eve they beat it with a stone or hammer until its face was completely obliterated. They also stamped their feet, as if to crack Haman's head, and played musical instruments. Children born during the festival are usually named Esther, Purim, or Mordechai. A standard practice, when referring to a clever person, is to say that he or she was born on Purim (on account of Esther's wisdom); malicious people are nicknamed Haman (*Omon*).

Spring Festival (*Sheghme-Vasal/ Hamiyasali*)

This festival, called *Sheghme-Vasal* (the Spring Candle) in Dagestan and the northern Caucasus and *Hamiyasali* (the Night of Spring) in Azerbaijan, is peculiar to the Caucasian Jews and is the only one of their holidays which is not tied to the Hebrew calendar. Fire plays a special role in this festival. Young people in Dagestan customarily skip over a campfire and chant songs of supplication, asking to be

Willow branch traditionally brought home on Hoshana Rabbah after the morning service at the synagogue, Kuba, Azerbaijan, 2000

protected from the evil eye, their fields shielded from drought during the planting season, and their animals spared from the cattle plague. The campfire is lit on the site of an abandoned threshing floor in order to ensure that the coming year will be fertile. The Jews of Azerbaijan are said to light lamps to remove the spirits of their enemies from their houses. On the eve of the spring holiday, these spirits hover over the entire world and threaten to bring disaster upon the Jewish people. A song sung by young people of the community echoes the desire to be rid of these spirits: "The campfires, the campfires/ Spring's pinnacle/ The campfires, the campfires/ May the enemy live this year only."

Passover (*Nisonu*)

Passover customs, like those of all other Jewish festivals, underwent substantial changes in the course of time. According to evidence from the first half of the nineteenth century, the head of the family slaughtered a lamb or kid on Passover eve, collected the blood, and smeared it over the doorpost according to the biblical injunction: "They shall take of the blood, and put it on the two side-posts and on the lintel" (Exodus 12:7). Afterwards, the meat was braised and eaten with a bitter spice. *Matzah* (*ghoghol*) was eaten for six days only, in accordance with the biblical precept: "Six days shall you eat unleavened bread" (Deuteronomy 16:8).

Caucasian Jews made lengthy and careful preparations for the Passover festival. Accounts dating from the second half of the nineteenth century show that during the long winter evenings women started to make new clothes for the whole family. Well before Passover, members of the community joined together in preparations for the baking of *matzot*. They endeavored to grow the wheat themselves and, if this was not possible, the wheat was bought from non-Jewish neighbors to be stored in new earthenware jars and guarded from the rain. A month before Passover the wheat was carefully selected; flour-mills underwent a thorough overhaul; and millstones were scrubbed with a powder ground from broken crockery. After the cleansing process a rabbi checked the result, and it was only on receipt of his approval that milling the wheat could begin. While the grain was being taken to the mill and the flour brought from there, any exposure to the sun was avoided to prevent fermentation.

Women did not participate in the baking of *matzah*. This duty was performed by fifteen to twenty men, each of whom was assigned a specific task: one weighed the flour, another measured the water, a third made the dough in small portions to insure that it did not become leavened (*hametz* in Hebrew), a fourth cut the dough into flat cakes, and an "expert" checked each stage of the procedure. They used cool pure water that had been set aside on the previous day and poured the right amount in one go, as the wrong quantity would render the dough unfit for use. The paddle with which they mixed the dough was constantly scraped with glass, to prevent the dough from sticking, and it was forbidden to lay it down while the work proceeded. Using a small iron cogwheel, they made Star-of-David perforations in the rolled dough and, as they worked, repeated the phrase: "This we do for the sake of the *matzah*." They baked the *matzah* in a new clay oven (*tenü* or *tendir*) which had never yet served to bake bread. In order to make it kosher for Passover, they heated the oven

Purifying vessels for
Passover, Kuba, Azerbaijan,
1996

Jewish women at the
cemetery on the 9th of Av,
Kuba, Azerbaijan, 1999

several times, bringing it to a high temperature. This process was known as *ogholo* (scalding). The bakers were careful not to let the *matzah* swell; returning *matzah* to the oven after its premature removal was strictly forbidden. During the 1960s, people began ordering *matzot* from families that specialized in its production; more recently, people have started to buy ready-made *matzah* from synagogues which handle the entire baking process.

The tradition of making the home ready for Passover has not changed over the past century. Caucasian Jews insist on the spring-cleaning of their house, which includes whitewashing all the walls and cleaning carpets and mattresses in the river or the yard. Those who can afford to do so buy new kitchenware for Passover. Metal items, widely used in the region, are given a new coating of tin and families that specialize in this work are kept busy during the month before the festival. No vessels are deemed kosher until they have been rinsed in boiling water. The practice in Dagestan is to immerse vessels in a cauldron of boiling water that also contains white-hot stones for raising the temperature. A different process is customary in Azerbaijan, where ashes (*xokisker*) replace hot stones in the cauldron, and the vessels to be immersed are filled with old glassware and earthenware; after immersion, the vessels are rinsed in cold water.

On the day before Passover, several related families join together and purchase a cow slaughtered by a rabbi. On the morning before Passover, women (and not men, as was usual in the past) collect all leavened food (*hamis*) and hand it over to the men, who throw it into the river or (according to a more recent practice) burn it. Only after disposal of the *hametz* can the women begin to prepare the festive meal. Families make an effort to send food items and clothing to needy members of the community before the holiday begins.

On Passover eve (*shev-nisonu*), the extended family assembles in the father's house (*xunei bebei*). Neighbors sometimes come to join them on the first night of Passover, when the *haggadah* (the liturgical text recounting the exodus from Egypt) is recited in Hebrew, as there are families in which no one can read Hebrew. On the second night the *haggadah* is recited in Tat.

On the night of the feast, a hard-boiled egg, boiled potatoes, and *haroset* (*hasurut*, a condiment made of apples and nuts) are placed on the festive table. *Qesni-boruxoi*, a local bitter herb, and *jurmesek-boruxu-odoma*, a plant eaten while it is still fresh and not covered with thorns, adorn the central plate. The Jews of Dagestan make their own red wine and sell it to their brethren in Azerbaijan. For the main course they prepare a dish known as *eshkene* (in Azerbaijan) or *yaghni* (in Dagestan) – meat soup with potatoes to which whisked eggs are added. Only the Jews of Dagestan set a wine-filled cup for Elijah the Prophet (*peile-Eliyahu*) on the table, and everyone drinks from it after the meal. The front door of the house is left open, as on Sabbaths and other festivals, to give poor people or wayfarers a chance to come in and join the festive meal.

In Dagestan, a piece of *matzah* serves as *afikoman* (traditionally hidden at the beginning of the meal; the child who finds it exchanges it for a present). In Azerbaijan, a hard-boiled egg wrapped in a cloth and tied onto the youngest child's back serves as *afikoman*. Whoever finds the egg can eat it the next morning. Preserves for the winter are not eaten during the festival. Rice, though deemed unsuitable for Passover, is eaten from the third day of the festival. On the morning of the first day, children go from house to house paying their respects and receive nuts, *matzah*, or eggs. From the third day onward, members of the community visit families in their year of mourning.

On the last day of Passover, trips are made into the countryside. In remembrance of the exodus from Egypt, this day is called *Gov'il-govlei* (Redemption): girls dress in traditional attire (*gobo*), form parties, and go out walking unaccompanied by their brothers. This offers young men the opportunity to choose a bride. On arriving home in the evening, they gather *mirbori*, a local type of herb, and throw it into the stove as a good omen presaging wealth. After supper, the young man's family visits that of the girl to ask for her hand in marriage.

Shavu'ot (*'Asalte*)

The name *'Asalte* (Festival of Honey) for Shavu'ot is only found among the Caucasian Jews and its origin is obscure. During the first half of the nineteenth century, Jewish elders still maintained the practice of collecting a tithe from the community's members between the New Moon of Nisan and Shavu'ot. Then, on Shavu'ot, they climbed to the top of a mountain and left the tithe there. The rest of the community followed, burning incense, singing songs, and lighting bonfires; sheaves of the new harvest's barley were thrown into the fire and portions of the Torah were read. At that time Shavu'ot was only celebrated as a one-day harvest festival on the biblical pattern (Exodus 23:16).

By the end of the nineteenth century, however, Shavu'ot had been associated with the Giving of the Law and its celebration lasted for two days. The "Festival of Honey" designation was now linked with the Torah's comparison of the land of Israel to milk and honey (Song of Songs 4:11). On the first night of Shavu'ot, rabbis and Torah scholars congregated in the synagogue, where passages from the Torah and Prophets were read as they drank wine and tea. The next morning people immersed themselves in the *mikveh* (ritual bath) adjoining the synagogue and resumed their prayers; the 613 Commandments were recited in the course of the day.

In the second half of the twentieth century, it has become the practice to decorate Jewish homes with flowers and plants in readiness for the holiday. Women bake a special kind of bread (*fadi*) made with butter; before the dough is baked in the oven, deep incisions are made into it with a bundle of feathers. For the meal of Shavu'ot eve, a rice-and-milk pudding with raisins and dill is prepared, and served with a dill-flavored pancake. The first fruits of the season (such as cherries) are placed on the table, as well as a vegetable salad or a large selection of fresh vegetables. Meat dishes are usually eaten on the second day. After the Scroll of Ruth is read in synagogue, one light is kindled for the entire congregation.

Tish'ah be-Av (*Suruni*)

The Caucasian Jews have several designations for the three weeks of public mourning between 17 Tammuz and the 9th of Av. Some call this period *suruni*, meaning "destruction," while others use the term *ruzoi ovul*, "Days of Mourning." Jews in the town of Vartashen call it *qatil*, "weeping" or "lamentation." As in all other Jewish communities, no festivities are held during this time; people also abstain from meat and hard liquor. It is customary to visit families in their year of mourning. On the day preceding Tish'ah be-Av (*me'alumei-suruni*), women make a special kind of bread (*nunoi tuti*) from dough whipped in butter, which is eaten together with cheese and cucumber. Beans are served before the beginning of the fast and after it ends.

Reports from the second half of the nineteenth century regarding Tish'ah be-Av mourning customs relate that men gathered in the synagogue, which remained in darkness. Worshipers sat on the floor; the community's rabbi recited the book of Jeremiah and the Scroll of Lamentations in a tearful voice. Congregants repeated the verses, beating their breasts, and many rubbed ashes on their forehead and went barefoot. During the day, people visited the burial ground to say *kaddish* (prayer for the dead), returning to the synagogue to read the books of Job and Jeremiah. On Tish'ah be-Av, Caucasian Jews now living in Israel, Germany, or the United States return to their hometowns to pay visits to the graves of their relatives.

---

1   This chapter is based on written evidence from a work by the Reverend Joseph Samuel, who
      visited the Caucasian Jews in 1837, documenting the early nineteenth century (I am grateful to
      Dr. Rivka Gonen for drawing my attention to this book); articles published in 1886–87, relating
      to the second half of the nineteenth century; and field work carried out during the second half
      of the twentieth century.
2   The links with Eastern-European Jewry were further tightened in the nineteenth century, after Russia
      annexed regions of the Caucasus that were populated by Mountain Jews.
3   *Kapparot* (expiation in Hebrew) is a custom according to which the sins of a person are symbolically
      transferred to an animal, usually a chicken. The chicken is swung around the head three times, and is
      thought to take on any misfortune that might befall the person in punishment of his sins.
4   The term "religious place," which occurs in the Book of Samuel, presumably alludes to the
      synagogue or its adjoining courtyard.

Bridal attendants at a
wedding party in the bride's
home, Azerbaijan, 1933
Photo courtesy of Beth Hatefutsoth,
The Nahum Goldmann Museum of
the Jewish Diaspora, Tel Aviv

The Life Cycle
Liya Mikdash-Shamailov

Birth and Circumcision

Numerous children were considered a blessing by Mountain Jews and by the peoples of neighboring cultures, and mothers of large families were highly esteemed. While two to three children has become the norm for most urban families in recent years, the average number of children in rural families is still five to six. In the past, abortions were considered a sin, and the community would renounce a woman who had one. Even a miscarriage was viewed unfavorably, and the woman was deemed partly responsible for the event.

The local rules of etiquette required that women conceal their pregnancy. Though there were no special maternity clothes, the apron that all women wore daily "protected" them by hiding a pregnancy from the eyes of strangers.[1] At home, however, the pregnant woman received a great deal of care and attention. The entire family, including the husband, provided assistance, freeing her from all strenuous work, indulging her with a variety of foods, and endeavoring to fulfill her every wish. Thus, if she found the aroma of her neighbor's cooking particularly enticing, her family would bring her some of the food to sample. This custom, named *bui varafde* (to bring forth an aroma), originates in the belief that if a pregnant woman's desires are not satisfied, she may give birth to a child with blue or green eyes – colors identified with the evil eye.[2]

Before the mid-twentieth century, women gave birth at home because of the shortage of doctors and hospitals. A midwife (*momo*) customarily attended women during labor and cared for babies after circumcision. Women gave birth standing, crouching on their knees, or, at times, lying on the ground. There was a tremendous difference between the reaction to the birth of a boy and that of a girl. The birth of a boy was greeted with great joy and provided a reason to give the midwife a generous gift; the birth of a girl was considered an affront to the family, especially the father.

The mother spent the first week after the birth in bed. For the first three days, she was not served meat. Instead, *xeshil* was prepared for her – a dish made from flour fried in butter and served with honey. Based on the Jewish law, the woman was considered impure for sixty days following the birth of a daughter and forty days following the birth of a son. At the end of this period, she went to be ritually purified by immersion before resuming conjugal relations with her husband.

The mother's parents showered the baby with presents – clothing, a cradle, gold jewelry, and rugs. An especially grand celebration called *gufere gushe* (*gufere* = cradle, *gushe* = accessory)

Circumcision tray and tools,
Kuba, Azerbaijan, 1950s
Silver, enamel, stainless
steel
D 27.6
Lent by Rabbi Eliezer Mizrahi,
Carmiel

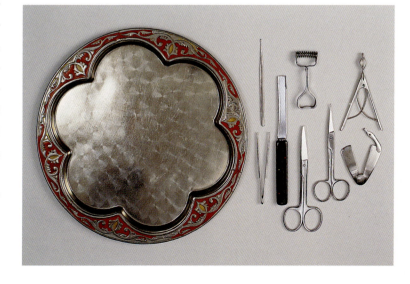

was held in honor of the birth of a first-born son. Relatives and friends invited to the celebration organized a joyous musical procession that started at the home of the mother's parents and ended at the home of the young couple.

If a circumcision took place on a Monday, Thursday, or Saturday, days on which the Torah is read publicly, then the ceremony was held in the synagogue. On other days, the ceremony took place at

home and was usually attended by musicians. It was viewed as a great honor to nurse the baby prior to circumcision, and every nursing woman present tried, at least, to draw the baby close to her breasts. If the ceremony was held in the synagogue, it was also considered a great honor to carry the baby to the Elijah's Chair. Though there were no carpenters among the Mountain Jews, they tried to construct this chair by themselves. The male relatives from both sides of the family stood in a line, forming a symbolic chain of generations, and passed the baby from hand to hand. A man in mourning stood in the next-to-last place. If no such person were present, the mother's grandfather took this

position and handed the baby to the godfather. The father's grandfather served as godfather, unless a great-grandfather from either side were still alive. If the ceremony took place at home, where there was no Elijah's Chair, the midwife was sent to bring one pillow from the chair in the synagogue, and the baby was placed upon it. The baby wore stockings with ribbons that were tied to the pillow. Families in mourning received a special invitation to the circumcision ceremony, and if they attended, they were thought to have done a very good deed.

The choice of the baby's name was of particular significance. Today it is still customary to honor the memory of a deceased relative by giving the new offspring his or her name. It is also common to name a child for a living relative, especially one from the father's side. Until twenty to thirty years ago, Jews gave only biblical names to their children; today, Muslim, Russian, and European names are also commonly given.

When a baby's first tooth appears (especially if the baby is a boy), a ceremony known as *gendume dush* (to cook wheat) is held. The baby's grandmother cooks a dish from wheat, lentils, beans, rice, and beef shank flavored with nuts and onions, which is distributed to neighbors and relatives in the belief that just as the ingredients are softened in the cooking, so the baby's gum will soften and let through the tooth without pain.

In the past, Mountain Jews did not conduct bar mitzvah ceremonies for thirteen-year-old boys. However, these celebrations were sometimes incorporated into the wedding ceremonies of first-born sons.

Baby's garment for the circumcision ceremony, Azerbaijan, 20th century
Cotton
L 31
Lent by Frieda Yosifov, Acre

Marriage

Despite attempts by the Soviet regime to erase the distinctive features of its member nations and homogenize them into a single Russian model, and despite the gradual abandonment of their traditional lifestyle, most Mountain Jews have retained customs connected with establishing a family.

A man who aspires to a prominent position in the community must establish a family. If he does not, he cannot carry a dagger in the scabbard of his belt or wear a hat, both symbols of the mature man in the Caucasian mountains.

Traditionally, all marriages were arranged. Most families employed a professional matchmaker (*ilche*), a mature woman respected by the community. Matchmaking was sometimes performed by the families themselves at a much earlier stage, before or shortly after their children were born. Occasionally, a girl was betrothed and conveyed to her future husband's family at the age of seven or eight, several years shy of the permissible age for marriage – twelve years and a day. She would assist her future mother-in-law in running the household and become accustomed to her new family.

The family of a man desiring to marry a particular young woman may have had to "kidnap" her if they knew that the bride's parents would not agree to the match. Such kidnappings were usually committed with the future bride's consent. Her parents' opposition was likely due to their dislike of the suitor's family or to the inability of the two families to agree on a bride price (*raḥ puli* in Azerbaijan, *hublary* in Kabardino-Balkaria). A kidnapping always disgraced the bride's family, especially her father and brothers, who were seen as incapable of safeguarding her honor. In most cases, the community council arranged a reconciliation between the two sides.

Mountain Jews tried to arrange marriages for their children within their own community or family. Marriages among cousins were accepted and very common. (Today, a professional matchmaker arranges most contacts, usually after a young man indicates that he is interested in a particular young woman, and it is still unusual for a couple to become personally acquainted on their own initiative.) The matchmaker, employed by the groom's family, approached the bride's family to assess their willingness. Even if the bride's parents were interested in the proposed match, they would likely give an evasive answer as a test to determine if the future in-laws had serious intentions.

A very formal atmosphere presided over the visit of the groom's parents to the bride's parents. Although refreshments were offered, the groom's family did not touch even a glass of water until an

Elijah's Chairs used in the circumcision ceremony, one for the godfather and one for Elijah the Prophet (reconstruction)
Fabrics covering the chairs lent by the Haifa Museum of Ethnology

Civil marriage ceremony of a
Jewish couple at the Baku
municipality, Azerbaijan,
1977
Photo courtesy of Esther Mikdash,
Kuba

affirmative answer to the proposed match was given. Negotiations usually focused on the bride price. In the past, the price was a fixed sum. The father of a groom in the nineteenth century, for example, gave the bride's father one cow, 288 kilograms of wheat, forty-eight kilograms of burgul, twenty hens, approximately three meters of silk, and one white sheet. Over the years, the guidelines became more flexible and the sum of the bride price negotiable. Two factors affected the bargaining: the economic status of the groom's parents and the bride's appearance and personal attributes. Half of the amount agreed upon was usually delivered when the match was settled.

After the match was arranged and before the wedding, a betrothal ceremony (*qidushi*; *kiddushin* in Hebrew) was held, during which the two parties signed the betrothal contract (*tonoi besde*), specifying the remainder of the bride price to be paid, the date of the marriage, the gifts the groom's family would offer, and so forth. Different communities hosted different kinds of betrothal ceremonies, and these changed in character over the years. For example, until about forty or fifty years ago, the betrothal ceremony in Dagestan was held without the groom. His parents covered the bride's head with a scarf and presented her with a ring or silver coin. The betrothal ceremony in Azerbaijan includes a substantial part of the marriage ceremony: the rabbi reads the terms of the marriage contract, the seven benedictions are recited, and the groom covers the bride's head. The bride and groom drink from the cup of wine and exchange rings (not a common Jewish custom), and the bride is presented with silver coins. The cup is not broken at this ceremony, and any vessel accidentally broken that day is viewed as a bad omen. During the actual wedding, the couple does not stand under a *huppah* (wedding canopy), but the ceremony is always held under a roof.

Following the ceremony, the groom's parents traditionally invited their future daughter-in-law to their home to get acquainted. After a week, she returned to her parents' house. A festive musical procession with many participants was organized every holiday and Sabbath eve between the betrothal and the wedding ceremonies. The procession, *tebeq ovurde* (to carry trays), takes its name from the trays – heaped with candy, clothing, jewelry, and gifts from the groom's family to the bride – that were carried by the groom's female relatives on their heads. In the past twenty years, the procession has become part of the betrothal ceremony rather than a separate event.

On the Sabbath and holidays, gifts (mainly candy) were bestowed upon the bride, and she distributed them to neighbors and relatives in a ceremony called *bexshei tebeqo* (gift trays). Until about fifty years ago, the bride would prepare a gift for the groom – a tobacco pouch or embroidered or beaded skullcap. The couple met for the first time in the period between the betrothal and the marriage. Friends of the bride and groom would chaperone the first meeting, known as *nimkurde vozi* (the betrothal game). While this custom still exists in small villages, young couples in large cities often arrange to meet without chaperones.

The date of the wedding was determined about a month in advance, after the groom's family finished paying the bride price. It was customary to visit relatives in mourning during this period and seek their consent for the marriage, which was always given. Preparations for the wedding started with the cutting of the material for the dress, a ceremony called *bulshei* or *burshei bura*. A small number of female relatives went to the dressmaker, bringing some sweets with them, and formally ordered the dress (*bulshei* or *burshei 'arusi*). The groom's parents also ordered clothes for their female relatives, a custom known as *bexshe*. The family also made a special effort to sew clothes for the poor, using the same pieces of material, and woolen shawls were presented to elderly women. In villages, nearly all members of the community, including Muslim neighbors, were invited to the wedding so as to avoid offending anyone.

The head chef (*keivoni*) played a very important role in organizing the wedding. A woman was honored with this position because of her ability to prepare a meal efficiently with the assistance of a few relatives. An invitation was sent to these relatives in the form of an apron and candle – the apron symbolized a request to "watch over the pots" (*ser qezqu*) and the candle, a request to "accompany the bride" (*epeser 'arus rafde*). The custom of honoring a woman to be head chef continues to this day.

The wedding parties lasted between four to ten days, depending on the financial situation of the groom's father, and they usually commenced on a Wednesday night. The bride began by visiting first-degree relatives and by inviting her female peers to provide her with a "healthy shoulder" (*soqdushi*), accompany her at the wedding ceremony, and provide assistance after the ritual immersion. Since the community did not have a *mikveh* (ritual bath), the bride immersed herself in a river after having washed at a bathhouse.

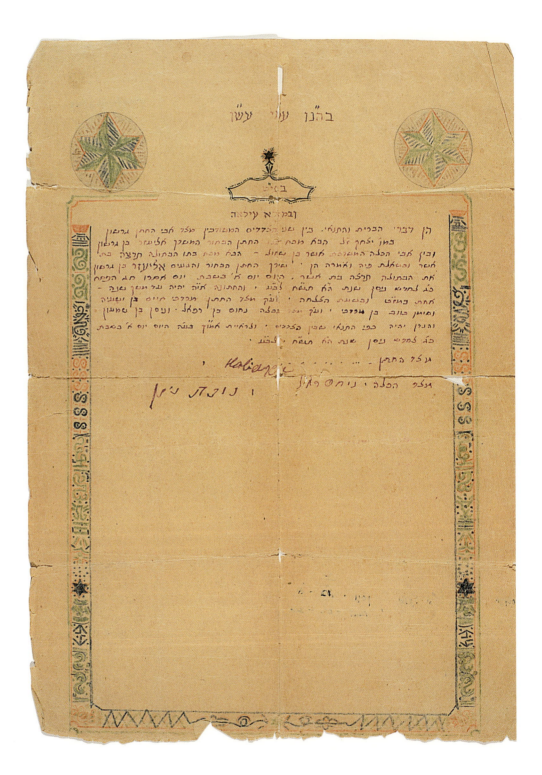

Engagement contract, Baku,
Azerbaijan, 1948

Opposite:
Ketubbah, Baku, Azerbaijan,
1949

The groom: Eliezer,
son of Gershon
The bride: Tirtza,
daughter of Asher

Ink on paper, colored
pencils
H 38; W 28

Courtesy of Rabbi Eliezer Mizrahi,
Carmiel

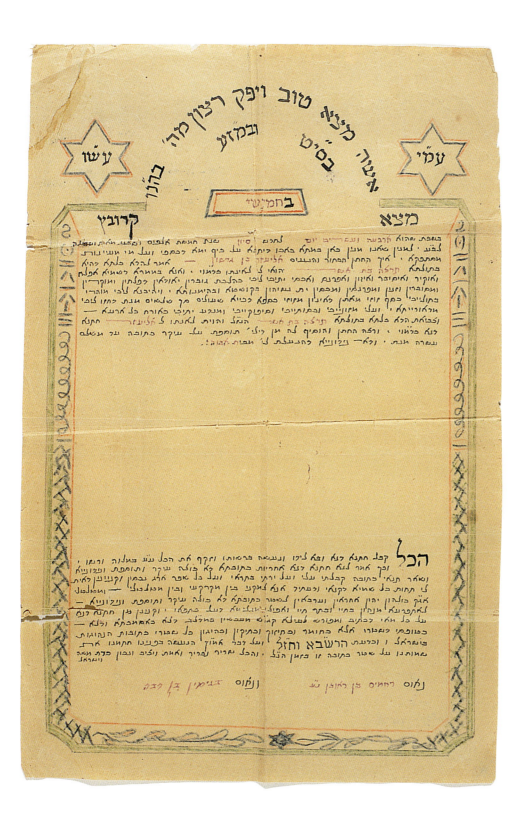

In every community, it was customary for guests to gather at the home of the bride's parents late in the afternoon on Wednesday, the first day of the wedding festivities. They brought presents for the bride, partook of a festive meal, and celebrated with song and dance. When the festivities ended at daybreak on Thursday, the henna ceremony was prepared. First a needle (to ward off the evil eye) and a silver coin (symbolizing wealth) were placed on a plate containing henna paste. (Recently an Israeli coin has been used to signify the connection to the land of the forefathers.) The henna was rubbed on the bride's hands and feet, and the plate was then passed to the guests, who dipped their fingers in the paste. The bride's brothers put the plate on a tray and passed it around so that guests could place money on it. In Azerbaijan, an additional ceremony, the *benigoru* (from the local Persian for "to say" or "to remind"), followed the henna ceremony. It was accompanied by a slow, melancholy melody and commenced with a reference to the land of Israel and the destruction of the Temple. The participants then sang: "*E benigoru, benigoru 'arus ne ḥatonish benigoru*" ("See, as I tell you about and remind you of the bride and groom"). Following the song, the names of all relatives, living and deceased, were recited, and the ceremony ended with another reference to the land of Israel and the destruction of the Temple. On that same night, the first night of the wedding, the groom and his first-degree male relatives attended a second *benigoru* ceremony, called *biror-domor* (friends of the groom), a gathering for men only at the groom's home.

On Thursday, the second day of the wedding, a barber came to cut the groom's hair and that of his friends before their ritual immersion in the river. When they emerged from the water, they competed in horseback-riding exercises. Later, they dressed the groom in his wedding outfit, placed ashes on his head in remembrance of the destruction of the Temple, and read Psalm 137 in a mournful melody. At this time, the parents of the bride and groom, the rabbi, and a few relatives met at the bride's house to write the *ketubbah* (*ketubo*), the marriage contract, which specified the contents of the dowry. Prior to the Soviet Revolution, printed *ketubbot* from the land of Israel were used. Several decades later, when diplomatic relations with Israel were severed, couples received simple, undecorated handwritten *ketubbot*. The bride's father arbitrarily determined the extent of the dowry and he decided what portion of the bride price it would include. He could also decide that his daughter would join the new family with no dowry. All items included in the dowry were brought to the groom's house in a slow procession, so that passers-by could take a good look at them and have the opportunity to praise (or criticize) the bride's parents.

Huppah customs varied among the different communities. In Dagestan, the young couple met in the synagogue courtyard for the *huppah* ceremony, which included the traditional breaking of the glass. Following most ceremonies, a procession of relatives carried candles and accompanied the bride to the house of the groom's family. The *yenge*, a female relative chosen to teach the young bride the secrets of intimacy prior to her first night with her husband, carried a lamp and led the procession. The bride's brother carried a mirror, which symbolized purity. The communities of Azerbaijan, as already mentioned, included most of the wedding ceremony in their betrothal ceremonies, and on the wedding day itself the couple did not go to the synagogue. The groom, along with a group of relatives, came to the bride's house to "redeem" her from her brothers, who guarded the door of her room. The *yenge* and the

Printed and gilt *ketubbah*,
Azerbaijan, 1974
The groom: Pa'ar'ez,
son of Avraham
The bride: Miriam, daughter
of Avrum
Paper
H 40; W 24.5
Lent by the Gross family, Tel Aviv

bride's brother, who also carried a mirror, then brought the bride to the groom's house. Passers-by would obstruct the procession (raḥ bura) several times and the grooms' friends would "redeem" the right to proceed for a symbolic amount of money. As the procession approached the groom's house, the couple was showered with rice, candy, and small coins. The entire procession wound its way to

the house of the groom's parents, where a festive nuptial meal had been prepared. The groom's mother greeted the bride with a plate of honey ('asal), into which the bride dipped her right hand. She then let her mother-in-law and father-in-law lick her honey-dipped hand, wiping the remainder on the doorframe in order to ensure a sweet and prosperous family life.

Until about fifty years ago, the bride did not participate in the festive nuptial meal. She and her chaperones were served food in a separate room, where a beautiful shawl (ḥüche) concealed the bridal bed. A young woman who had married in the past year was invited to join the group as a symbol of the new bride's entrance into adult society and the community. The groom sat on the floor in the largest room of the house, next to a silk scarf on which were piled the gifts he had received – money and silver and gold objects – from guests and family (including his mother). A relative stood nearby to present the gifts and announce the names of the givers. When all the gifts had been received, they were itemized, with witnesses, and then became the groom's property. During the 1970s, marriage customs underwent change. The young couple began to participate in the festive gatherings, and the presents and money brought by guests became the possession of the groom's parents.

After the young couple danced, the bride was accompanied to the bedroom. Before joining her, the groom bowed down before his parents and kissed their hands as a sign of his total submission. Some time after the groom left his nuptial bed, the yenge would enter the room. When she left, she held a blood-soaked handkerchief in her hand, proof of the bride's virginity and a sign that she had become a member of the family (duxter hune). The handkerchief was given to the groom's friends (biror-domor) who, together with the yenge, guarded the bedroom door. The groom's friends then took the handkerchief to the bride's father, who "redeemed" it from them. In the past, if the bride could not prove her virginity in this manner, the celebrations immediately ceased, her braid was cut off, and she was dressed in male clothing, put on a donkey facing his tail, and led back to her parents' house. Today, these brides are simply sent home, and the groom demands that the bride price he paid for her be returned.

During the first week of the marriage, a baby or child (sometimes the bride's brother or sister) would be put between the couple in their bed in order to prevent them from having conjugal relations, which the laws of niddah (ritual impurity) prohibited. At the end of the week, the child received presents and was returned home. Within the first forty days after the wedding, the groom's parents hosted the bride's family at their home for the Sabbath, thereby giving the young bride an opportunity to "show her face" (rui vokunde). Until she had her first child, the young woman received

A bride wipes her honey-dipped hand on the doorpost of her groom's house in order to ensure a prosperous life, Acre, 1998
Photo courtesy of Regina Agarunov, Moscow

food for the Sabbath from her parents. Only after the birth of her first child (and especially if the child were male) would her husband's family totally embrace her.

Divorce was a rare event among Mountain Jews. A woman's infertility sometimes provided grounds for divorce, but the husband usually chose to take a second wife instead. Before the 1920s,

the community of Mountain Jews did not accept the ban on polygamy enacted in the Middle Ages by Gershom ben Yehudah. Bigamy was practiced among wealthy people and rabbis, even if their first wives were not barren. In this kind of marriage, each woman ran her own household.

Levirate marriages (*yibum*), in which a man is obligated to marry his brother's widow if she is childless, and *halitzah*, the ceremony releasing this couple from their obligation to marry, were customary in the community of Mountain Jews. They were also performed when a groom died between his betrothal and his marriage. The *halitzah* ceremony in the Caucasus, unlike that of other communities, could fail to take effect. Special significance was attached to the way that

the knots on the shoelaces were untied during the ceremony. If the widow managed to untie them, all ties with her deceased husband's family were severed; if she did not succeed, she was not permitted to remarry ever. In order to prevent the latter situation, a unique solution evolved within the community, whereby the deceased husband's brother would fulfill the precept of levirate marriage, but both sides agreed that the marriage would only last several months. During this time, his family tried to insure the widow's future by providing financial support and even finding a new match. At the end of this brief period, the widow was divorced and free to marry any man she wished. At the end of World War II, when many soldiers did not return, levirate marriages became commonplace. Since then, *yibum* and *halitzah* are no longer practiced by Mountain Jews, and women who are childless when their husbands die are considered ordinary widows. In the past, it was also common for a Jewish widower to marry the sister of his deceased wife.

Other changes in marriage customs have occured in recent years. Today, no couples marry without having previously met each other. The wedding need not begin on a Wednesday, and the celebration lasts for two days – one at the bride's house and one at the groom's. In addition, it is no longer customary to go to the river for ritual immersion; the bathhouse serves as a substitute.

Marriages between young people from different villages or cities, previously very rare, have also increased in number. Though child marriages are no longer performed, there are betrothal ceremonies for girls of sixteen or seventeen, still below the marriageable age according to civil law. Religious ceremonies are held for underage brides, and civil registration is postponed until they reach the age

Tray of fruit arranged in a Star-of-David pattern for the wedding, Kuba, Azerbaijan, 1996

of eighteen. The custom of paying a bride price continues, but the wedding expenses (including the groom's wedding outfit) are now paid for by the bride's family. A rabbi officiates at the betrothal and wedding ceremonies, which are held at home and not at the synagogue. The young couple now freely meets between the engagement and the marriage. In some communities, it is customary for their friends to join them in the first meeting. The requirement concerning the bride's virginity has not changed. In addition to performing religious ceremonies, Mountain Jews now register their marriages with the civil authorities and lay wreaths of flowers upon monuments to soldiers killed in World War II. Until about fifty years ago, intermarriages were very rare, and the few that took place were between Jewish men and non-Jewish women. Such marriages were considered a great blow to the family. Intermarriage today is still very rare among the Jews of the Caucasus.

Burial and Mourning Customs

Ceremonies connected with the dead play a prominent role in the community of Mountain Jews. Accordingly, numerous customs reflect a special sensitivity to the bereaved family during the first year of mourning. Condolence calls are paid on Fridays and Saturdays. Family relations and friends

A Jewish man with his two
wives, Buinaksk, Dagestan,
1926
Photo courtesy of Avraham
Avrahamov, Tel Aviv

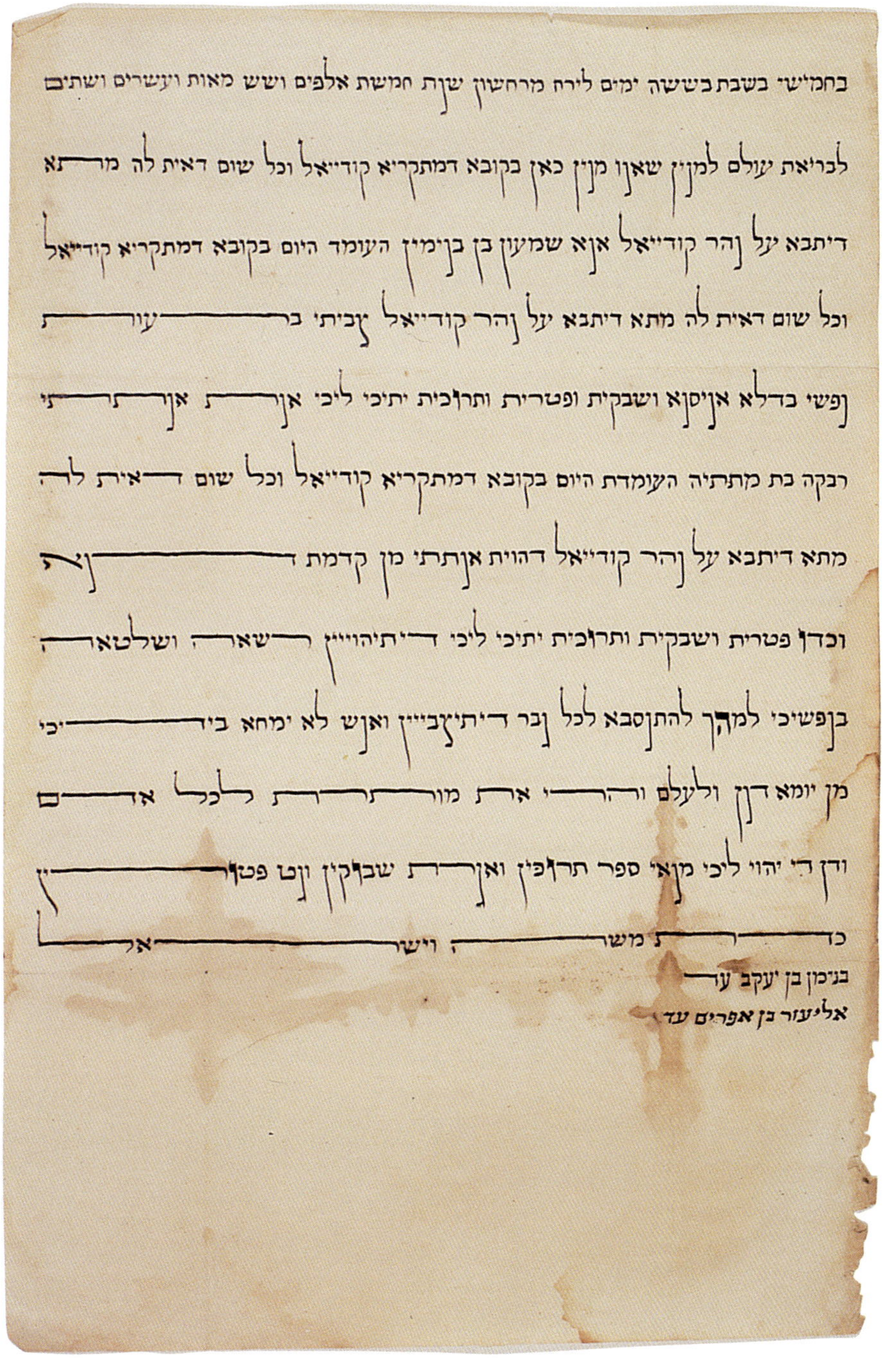

בחמישי בשבת בששה ימים לירח מרחשון שנת חמשת אלפים ושש מאות ועשרים ושתים

לבריאת עולם למנין שאנו מנין כאן בקובא דמתקריא קודייאל וכל שום דאית לה מר——תא

דיתבא יעל נהר קודייאל אנא שמעון בן בנימין העומד היום בקובא דמתקריא קודייאל

וכל שום דאית לה מתא דיתבא יעל נהר קודייאל צביתי בר——————עור

נפשי כדלא אניסנא ושבקית ופטרית ותרוכית יתיכי ליכי אנ——ת אנ——תי

רבקה בת מתתיה העומדת היום בקובא דמתקריא קודייאל וכל שום ד——אית לה.

מתא דיתבא יעל נהר קודייאל דהוית אנתתי מן קדמת ד——נא

וכדו פטרית ושבקית ותרוכית יתיכי ליכי דיתיהוייין ר—שאה ושלטאה

בנפשיכי למהך להתנסבא לכל גבר דיתיצבייין ואנש לא ימחא ביד——יכי

מן יומא דנן ולעלם והרי——י ארת מור—תר—רת ליכל אר———

ודן די יהוי ליכי מנאי ספר תרוכין ואג—רת שבוקין וגט פטו——

כד—ר—ת משר——————ת וישר—————אל

בנימן בן יעקב עד

אליעזר בן אפרים עד

Divorce certificate, Kuba,
Azerbaijan, 1862
Ink on paper
H 38; W 26
Lent by Abraham Frohlich,
Jerusalem

celebrating marriages or births visit a house of mourning to ask permission to perform a wedding ceremony or to extend a special invitation to a circumcision ceremony.

The centrality given to death in Caucasian society may explain why its burial and mourning customs have remained almost entirely unchanged. When a person's death becomes known, his or her home is visited not only by friends and relatives but also by strangers who come to pay their last respects. Verbal expressions of mourning, always initiated by women, resound loudly. All the female relatives — mother, wife, sisters, and daughters — cry out in a heartrending voice, scratching their skin and pulling out their hair. Professional, paid mourners (*girye soqdohor*) add their voices to those of the family in wailing (*girye*) over the deceased.

A group of five young men is organized to begin digging a grave shortly after the death is announced publicly. While the grave is being prepared, the body is placed on the floor or the earth in the home of the deceased, candles are lit, and the rabbi reads from the Book of Psalms and teaches chapters from the Mishnah. Once the grave has been dug, members of the *hevra kadisha* (Jewish burial society) wash the body. One of the children, sometimes chosen in accordance with the deceased's request, pours pure water (*ov ḥololi*) over the body for the last time for ritual purification. This ceremony can also be held in the courtyard of the home, in a tent erected especially for this purpose, or, more recently, in the bedroom of the deceased.

Kaddish (prayer for the dead) in Cyrillic script
Israel Museum Collection, gift of Azariah Isakov, Ashkelon

The shrouds (*axirati*) comprise a large sheet and a set of garments, all sewn by the women from a thin cloth. The garments – a shirt, trousers, stockings, skullcap, and gloves for men, and a dress and stockings for women – are sewn together so that they cover all parts of the body except for the face, which is covered by a separate cloth. The sheet is then wrapped over the clothes, and, in the case of men, a *tallit* (prayer shawl) is placed on top. Customarily, the sons of the deceased hang around their necks cloth straps made from the remnants of the material used to make the shrouds. If the deceased reached a ripe old age – more than ninety years – the strips of leftover material are punched with holes and hung from the backs of children as amulets for longevity.

Burial customs for people who were killed differ somewhat from those for people who died a natural death. They are buried on the day they were killed, with no ritual purification. They are wrapped in shrouds on top of their own clothing. If they carried a weapon, it is customary to bury it along with the body.

When preparations for burial are completed, the body is laid out on a stretcher. Six people carry the stretcher, and every twenty-five to thirty steps the stretcher-bearers are changed. The funeral procession stops three times. Each time, the stretcher is lowered to the ground and the rabbi reads prayers. If the deceased was a religious functionary (*odomi nimaz*), the procession stops seven times. The final prayer is recited in front of the *hevra kadisha* building, located near the cemetery. As the procession approaches the grave, the stretcher-bearers change for the last time. The body is then lowered into the grave with its head pointing eastward and feet to the west (in the direction of Jerusalem), and earth is piled underneath the head. Wooden planks are placed around the body, and all in attendance help to cover the grave with earth. They do not pass the shovel from hand to hand but place it on the ground to be picked up by each person in turn.

Halfway to the cemetery, the women are sent home. Their task is to collect the water used to wash the body and take it away to dispose of it. They must also throw out any food left in the room occupied by the deceased and prepare the "recovery meal" (*boroxo*) before the men return. The composition of the meal changes in accordance with the age of the deceased and the circumstances of his or her death: If the deceased was young, or was murdered and bled before dying, no meat is served at the meal, only boiled potatoes, boiled eggs, apples, and dried fruit; if he or she was elderly, meat is served as well. If the deceased was more than a hundred years old and left numerous

Coffin for carrying the dead,
Oguz, Azerbaijan, 2000

Funeral procession walking from the home of the deceased to the cemetery, Kuba, Azerbaijan, 2000

descendants, the death is marked by a joyous celebration. The men in attendance, and later the women, dine upon the floor of the room where the deceased had lain.

Until the 1970s, each participant in the "recovery meal" would bring food. Recently, it has become customary to jointly pay for the food, and one of the relatives makes a list of participants and records the sum paid by each. This custom is one means of providing economic assistance for the deceased's family. When the men return from the cemetary, one of the family members takes a cup of water outside and pours it over their hands. They then place their wet hands on their faces.

During the *shivah* (*hofti*) period – the seven ritual days of mourning – relatives visit the synagogue twice a day, in the morning (for *shaharit* prayers) and in the afternoon (for *minha* and *ma'ariv* prayers). It is customary to gather at the grave on the seventh day and thank those who took part in the period of mourning. Close relatives remain at the deceased's house, sleeping there until thirty days after the death. In Azerbaijan this period is called *chule*, and in Dagestan *seim*. Following the thirty-day period of mourning and another visit to the grave, the relatives go to the bathhouse and change their clothing. The men also cut their hair. This ends the first stage of mourning.

In the first year of mourning, meals for the Sabbath eve and Sabbath day are held at the home of the deceased in the company of people paying condolence calls. During this period, relatives do not attend weddings or funerals; if they receive a special invitation to a circumcision

ceremony, however, their attendance is considered an important deed. If the deceased had no surviving family, all of his or her clothing is given to the synagogue. In the past, if a man died a short time before or after his marriage, his fiancée or wife and his sister used to cut off their braids and bury them with the deceased.

The tombstone is unveiled either on the thirtieth day or one year after death, in accordance with the family's financial situation. In the past, some communities destroyed the stretcher after burial in order to "stop the death"; other communities retained the stretcher to show that they "do not fear death." Today, all communities retain the stretcher, one of the few changes in traditional customs of mourning.

1   For a description of women's dress, see the chapter on dress and jewelry, p. 135.
2   For a discussion of this belief and others, see the chapter on beliefs and ceremonies, p. 111.

Paid mourners in the home
of Daniel Nuvahov, Kuba,
Azerbaijan, 1999

ויהְוָד
עִמּו

תבב תצמץ בוכו בתל בוכו יד יהבץ
נוכו יהוד מצפץ טרההד   כוזו
צבאות השתפא

אלי
ביונסים
אאצל יאר
ונחמצא חן בעי
פאי   יהור   חתו

מיכאל גבריאל

בשם שדי דיברא צמיא
וחרעצא בשם אהיה הקדוש תנפץ
אבינו כוזו מלכינו צמרכד
מלכינו יוצר בראשית תצמז
בוכו

Beliefs and Ceremonies
Liya Mikdash-Shamailov

The beliefs of the Mountain Jews have undoubtedly been influenced by those of the Caucasian peoples among whom they have lived for hundreds of years. Evil spirits and sorcery are the usual explanations for illnesses and other misfortunes. To counteract these forces, the Mountain Jews seek the help of fortune-tellers and healers, many of whom are Muslims, and consult with experts on the medicinal properties of regional plants. Beliefs and ceremonies involving magic have survived over many generations, and many still play a central role in the daily life of the Mountain Jews.

The Evil Eye

Belief in the evil eye is widespread among natives of the Caucasus. Members of the Jewish community attempt to neutralize its effect by carrying amulets prepared by rabbis or healers and often containing substances gathered from nature. One amulet used today by Jews of the Caucasus consists of a piece of dark fabric containing charcoal and grains of barley. It is usually attached to clothing, hidden from view on adults but prominently displayed on children. The evil eye can also be banished through Talmudic verses copied by sages in their own handwriting. The verses are suspended over a baby's cradle, along with beads made of natural materials, in a custom that blends aesthetics, magical practices, and religion.

Healers are thought to have the ability to understand and cure physical weakness, a condition usually attributed to the evil eye. One method they use is to throw balls of dough into a fire while calling out the names of all enemies known to the patient. If the balls burn without exploding or bouncing out of the fire, the evil eye is not to blame. If a ball explodes when the name of an enemy is called out, the healer must rip off a piece of the enemy's garment, burn it, let the patient inhale the smoke, and sprinkle the patient's forehead with the ash. The evil eye can also be thwarted by reading a glass of water. Wax or melted lead is tossed into the water, and the ensuing form is believed to closely resemble the person who caused the illness. Salt is then scattered over a fire, blinding – or even destroying – the enemy whose image was revealed. Yet another manner of causing injury to an enemy is to take a handful of earth from the grave of a relative of the enemy and sprinkle it on the enemy's bed.

Strings of beads composed of precious stones are thought to both prevent and cure illness: the red garnet protects against poisons and injuries; the purple amethyst helps to banish evil thoughts; the carnelian (whose color resembles that of raw meat) relieves toothaches and stops bleeding.

Mountain Jews who encounter people with blue or green eyes are likely to turn in the opposite direction. This custom is based on the belief that people who lack a sharp contrast between the white of the eye and the iris can unintentionally cast the evil eye. Mountain Jews also avoid arguing with old people who live alone, orphans, the poor, and the mentally ill, as their curses are deemed to possess great magical power: since these people are sheltered by the shadow of the Divine Presence,

Opposite:
Amuletic page from *Charms, Amulets, and Lots* by Reuven, son of Avraham Moshe, Kuba, Azerbaijan, 1861–66
Ink on paper
H 20.7; W 16.5
Lent by the Gross family, Tel Aviv

their curses travel a direct route to God. Loose hairs or nail clippings must never be tossed on the ground, since evil spirits may retrieve them for use in casting spells. Likewise, one should avoid stepping on other people's loose hairs or nail clippings. Reckless and hasty actions are also attributed to the influence of the evil eye.

The Spirits of Darkness and Imaginary Creatures

Although the Mountain Jews believe in the existence of one God, they also worship supernatural forces under God's dominion. These forces may be visible, and some take on the form of animals. They have the power to punish people for their sins and reward them for their good deeds. While some have permanent features, others change in appearance and character according to a person's behavior.

Necklace with amuletic pendant and Russian coins, Kuba, Azerbaijan, 20th century
Silver
Lent by Frieda Yosifov, Acre

Opposite:
Top: Leather pouch containing amuletic parchment, 20th century
H 5.2; W 8.7
Israel Museum Collection, gift of Malka Ilizarov, Kuba

Middle: Amulet incised with Hebrew formulas, Dagestan, 20th century
Silver
H 3.5; W 3.5
Lent by Gila Rubinov-Ya'akov, Holon

Bottom: Amulet for pregnancy incised with Hebrew formulas, 20th century
Silver
D 4.5
Lent by Abraham Frohlich, Jerusalem

When leaving on a long journey, especially late at night, the Mountain Jews usually take some sort of metal object with them. They are scrupulous in uttering the phrase "num-xudoi" ("in the name of God") in order to avoid any encounter with She'atu — an evil spirit that stirs in the dark and often appears in deserted houses, near water sources, in open fields, or in the thick of forests. She'atu is believed to be afraid of hot water. Members of a household are therefore forbidden to spill hot water, especially bath water, on the floor, since doing so may cause She'atu to go wild and inflict mental illnesses. When bathing their children, mothers must be sure to place a broom or metal object upon the basin of hot water in order to chase She'atu away. Pouring hot water outside the entrance of a house is, likewise, discouraged, since spirits are thought to dwell underground — particularly under the threshold of the house. Mountain Jews therefore avoid stepping directly on the threshold and do not linger there when greeting guests.

The spirit Num-ne-gir (literally, "she whose name shall not be uttered") is associated with fertility and familial happiness. She is also responsible for the safety of travelers. Her name remains unspoken because it inspires great fear. Though no one knows exactly what will trigger her anger, she can be appeased if one shows love for one's fellow human beings, love for children, and hospitality to strangers. Different types of encounters with *Num-ne-gir* can have very different effects: while a fleeting moment with her promises good fortune, familial happiness and children's well-being are endangered if she passes between a person's legs. *Num-ne-gir* may even attempt to strangle children, forcing parents to move to another place and "redeem" their offspring. The redemption ceremony resembles one performed to protect children born after the death of a sibling (see section on birth and child-rearing below).

The spirit of the Water Mother, *Ser-ovi* or *Dedei-ovi*, lures lovers or pregnant women to a river in which they disappear forever. Pregnant women are, therefore, advised not to leave their houses unaccompanied. Women in labor are also in danger and should not be left alone, since the Water Mother can take the shape of a relative, enter the woman's house, raise the blanket on her bed, and eat away at her entrails. If the Water Mother is apprehended in time and her hair cut, the woman's life can be saved. The spirit disappears if she looks at a steel ring.

Beliefs Connected with the Life Cycle

Marriage

Evil spirits are inclined to interfere with marriage ceremonies. Accordingly, at the start of the ceremony, immediately after the rabbi's first benediction, a woman in attendance (usually a relative of the bride or groom) begins to tie knots. The knots are believed to contain magical power that influences the groom's ability to approach his bride. The knot-tying must be done quickly and skillfully in order to preempt the enemies, who endeavor to break the newlyweds' union by tying their own knots. The woman must then untie her knots during the recitation of the seven benedictions so that the union of the bride and groom will be crowned with success. She must also be careful that the number of knots does not exceed nine, since this could shorten her own life.

Hammering nails is another way to thwart an evil effect on a couple's life. In recent times, locks and keys have also been employed. When the groom places the wedding ring on the bride's finger, relatives symbolically fasten the lock, and when the couple spends its first moments together as man and wife, the lock is opened.

Necklace with amuletic
pendant and Russian coins,
Azerbaijan, 20th century
Silver
L 26
Lent by Frieda Yosifov, Acre

Infertility

The reasons for a couple's infertility must be investigated. Their relatives determine if the knots tied by their enemies at the wedding ceremony were stronger than their own, or if there were unfortunate circumstances unknown that day. The reason may have been the presence at the wedding of a young woman who had been married less than forty days prior to the ceremony. If this is the case, a pretext is found to invite the "veteran" bride to visit the new bride, so that the latter may pass under the feet of her visitor.

Birth and Child-Rearing

Many magical ceremonies of the Mountain Jews are connected with birth and the rearing and education of children. When a woman experiences a difficult birth, her relatives usually rend their clothes or strike two stones together until they shatter. Rabbis come to the aid of families whose children died young by crafting

special silver rings for them, using coins collected from families with many children. Families with daughters but no sons receive from the rabbis rings made from coins collected from families with male offspring only. Biblical verses are inscribed on the underside of the ornament attached to the ring, and the woman is commanded to wear the ring for the rest of her life.

A long-awaited son born after the death of several siblings is usually wrapped in rags, left in an agreed-upon place, and subsequently "collected" by relatives. Some time later, the baby's parents "find" and redeem him from the relatives. The baby is then given a new name – *Shende* (literally, "thrown away") or *Ofdum* ("I found"). A similar ceremony is also held for a child threatened with strangulation by *Num-ne-gir.* The parents show the fates that they have already lost a child and should not be punished again. Until the child reaches the age of seven, a lock of hair in the middle of his head remains uncut. A festive meal is then prepared as a gesture of thanksgiving that the boy has passed the critical years of his life. Relatives and other honored guests attend the celebration. The rabbi cuts the child's lock of hair and receives his payment – the weight of the shorn lock in gold and silver. In the past, it is told, the lock of hair was sent to Jerusalem. On this occasion, an earring worn by the boy since infancy to deceive the evil spirit into thinking that he is a girl is removed.

Mountain Jews believe that one should not rock or cover the empty cradle of a baby since this could cause the baby to become ill or even die. Most place a metal object, Torah scroll, or clove of garlic in the empty cradle to chase away evil spirits. These methods are also used to protect a child left alone at home.

Clockwise from top:

Ring with amuletic parchment underneath its bezel, Dagestan, 20th century
Silver
D 2.3
Lent by Yafah Hilleli, Kiryat Bialik

Jewish girl wearing amulets, Kuba, Azerbaijan, 1999

Amuletic beads strung on a safety pin, Azerbaijan, 20th century
Clay, metal
L 6
Lent by the Haifa Museum of Ethnology

Amuletic pages from the
handwritten book *Charms,
Amulets, and Lots* by
Reuven, son of Avraham
Moshe, Kuba, Azerbaijan,
1861–66
Ink on paper
H 20.7; W 16.5
Lent by the Gross family, Tel Aviv

The Elements of Nature

Sky

Mountain Jews avoid pointing upwards to the sky, an action indicating contempt for God that may be punished by death. Perhaps the threat of this cruel fate explains why Jews are careful never even to point at other people. They also take care to swear "in the name of heaven" only in times of great distress and face the heavens when cursing their enemies.

The stars are seen as replicas of human souls. The Mountain Jews believe that when a baby is born a new star appears in the sky, and that when that person dies the star falls.

Thunder, Lightning, and Rain

Natural phenomena such as thunder and lightning are both feared and repected by the Mountain Jews. The first rains of spring are viewed as sacred; they grant the special qualities of grace and purity to the people and the land. Parents usually undress their little children and send them outside to run in the first spring rain. They believe that rainwater promotes hair growth and prevents skin disease, and they collect it to use for bathing as well.

Caucasian peoples, including the Jews, held magical ceremonies in order to restrain the forces of nature and prevent calamities — such as drought, hail, or rain — from interfering with their daily lives. One example is the *gudil* ceremony, which has two functions: to appeal for rain during a drought and to bring excessive rains to an end. Until recently, children in some regions marched in a noisy procession carrying a *gudil* figure — a scarecrow made of branches and rags. The procession wound its way past all the Jewish homes, where young women laughed and older women recited prayers. All distributed presents to the children and poured cold water on the scarecrow, hoping that the rain would similarly quench the land. On occasion, one of the adult members of the community, usually a poor person, would play the role of the *gudil*. He was completely covered with long branches so that he could not be recognized. In a parallel ceremony requesting sunshine when spring rains threatened the sowing of crops, the scarecrow was colored red and the prayers called for clear skies.

Fire

Fire is highly regarded by the Mountain Jews as a benevolent power that protects a household and also contains supernatural elements. Their views about fire may have been influenced by the Persian Zoroastrian religion. A Jew who wishes to impart additional force to an oath will say, "I swear by this fire." It is forbidden to throw certain objects into a fire: hair may contaminate it, onion peels are deemed "devil's tears" and can cause a family to lose its entire fortune, and bread can cause blindness. It is also forbidden to spit or throw water into a fire. Housewives extinguish lanterns with a careful breath. When cleaning their ovens of soot, they pile it separately from other waste so as not to contaminate fire (with which soot is associated).

Like many other peoples around the world, the Mountain Jews believe that fire plays an important role in purifying, intimidating, or banishing evil spirits. Two candles are lit at burial ceremonies and burn for seven days. Until recently, wedding processions were accompanied by burning torches; candles and oil lamps are used today.

Birds and Animals

The Mountain Jews are well known for their reverence of birds and animals. It is considered a great achievement to trap and keep a snake (*mar*) using a bait of sour milk or milk and honey, since the snake is in charge of a household's well-being. Folklore endows it with the traits of wisdom, honesty, nobility, and temperance, and it is a symbol of good luck and prosperity. According to tradition, the snake has the ability to return love, uncover deceit, and aid those who have treated it kindly. It also has the power to bestow wealth and create other positive turnabouts of fate. Families conceal the nesting site of this miraculous snake from strangers for fear that they will remove it or cast the evil eye on them for bringing such a creature into the house.

Attitudes toward swallows are ambivalent. Although their visits to porches and houses cause much inconvenience for housewives, it is considered a sin to destroy their nests or kill them. If a nest is found empty one year after the swallow's last visit to a home, the family can expect some mishap. However, if a swallow nests in the home of a *kohen* (a descendant of Aaron the High Priest), the family must move to another house; and if a swallow builds a nest in the new house, that house must be torn down. The explanation for this ambivalent attitude is rooted, on the one hand, in the Caucasian peoples' veneration of the swallow (which also influenced the Jews) and, on the other hand, in the need to reject Muslim tradition, which deems the swallow sacred since it comes from Mecca.

The dove, symbol of solitude and innocence, arouses special feelings. It is believed that the dove's wings can protect people from the fires of hell when they stand in judgement before God. Although the Mountain Jews cannot point to the source of these beliefs, their origin is apparently in the neighboring Muslim culture.

Plants

Magical properties are also attributed to plants, many of which are known for their medicinal properties. The Mountain Jews highly value the nut tree, which can prevent infertility and childhood diseases. One accepted belief is that by lingering for some time under a wild nut tree, people absorb the earth's beneficial powers and escape certain diseases. On the other hand, planting nut trees is not advised, and it is forbidden to sleep under one, especially at sunrise or sunset, since lightning is thought to strike nut trees more than other types. It is forbidden to chop down a nut tree so as not to anger the destructive spirits dwelling in its branches.

An efficient way to counteract the evil eye is to plant a cornel tree (*zugol*), known for its medicinal properties and ability to protect one from the evil eye. Its branches are used to manufacture especially sturdy agricultural tools, and the shape of its fruit inspires the design of decorative objects, jewelry, and amulets.

Sacred Objects in Nature

After living for hundreds of years in close proximity, the Jews of Azerbaijan and other peoples in the region came to view the same objects as sacred; these included trees, buildings, and rocks that had been struck by lightning and were believed to have the power to grant good fortune and protection against illness, infertility, and the evil eye. They also worshiped the peaks of tall mountains, natural piles of rocks, caves, and tombs and tombstones. They believed that by entering mountain crevices or wells dug at holy sites one could cleanse away sin. Some people, it was thought, had been granted the power to communicate with the spirits dominating the sacred sites and placate them through animal sacrifices or offerings of expensive objects. Earth taken from the sites was thought to contain curative properties when mixed with water and swallowed.

Stones found on mountain peaks that had been shaped in a special way as a result of being struck by lightning were used as amulets, and were customarily hung over the entranceway of a house.

I wish to express my appreciation to Rabbi Shende Moiseev, Mirbori Misheiv, Porat Aharonova, and Shoshan Mikdashiva for providing me with valuable information.

Healing through magic,
Kuba, Azerbaijan, 1999

Material
Culture

Daily Life in the Caucasus
Liya Mikdash-Shamailov

The Family

The family structure of Caucasian Jews was characterized by a strict patriarchal hierarchy that was maintained for centuries and only began to change in the early twentieth century. The extended family (*kele-kiflet*) consisted of three or four generations of first-degree relatives from the male side, and at times numbered up to seventy persons. The role of the head of the family (*bebe*) was handed down from father to eldest son; if the head of the family did not have any sons, the role passed to the next male relative. His authority over the extended family was absolute, and he took all the important decisions – arranged marriages, purchases, the division of property, and so on – without consulting other family members. He also had the unquestioned right to punish or reward any member of the family. No woman was entitled to lead the family, but the eldest woman (*kele-zen*), usually the wife of the head of the family, played a very important role in the extended family. She ran the household, and all the other women were subject to her authority. When she died, or if she lost her ability to function, the role was assumed by the wife of her firstborn son.

The extended family maintained a shared household, and all were obliged to contribute to the common good. Children below the age of twelve and the elderly were exempt from especially rigorous labors, which were generally reserved for the men – though the women too were heavily burdened: they took part in all the field labors except for plowing, ran the household, tended to the animals, and, during their free time, engaged in weaving, sewing, knitting, basket weaving, and other handicrafts. All the family property – livestock, buildings, precious rugs, jewelry, and eating utensils – was commonly owned, and was mainly acquired through the dowry paid for brides. The family's entire income, including the salaries of the sons who worked in the city, was entrusted to the head of the family, who decided on its allocation.

In the more distant past, the main meal of the day was prepared in the house of the father, but as the framework of the extended family weakened, the sons' families began to cook their meals separately, except on holidays and other festive occasions. The store of foodstuffs continued to be kept in one central location, and was apportioned among the sons' families as needed, under the supervision of the *kele-zen*. The institution of the extended family persisted in this form until the 1920s, and in a number of places such as the quarter of Krasnaya Sloboda in Kuba, until the 1950s. The process of family breakdown began after the October Revolution, as a result of the ensuing economic, social, and political changes. In most instances, the death of the head of the family accelerated the division within each family. The eldest son sought to continue the traditional way of life, while his brothers preferred to disband the extended family and take their share of the common property. Families that relinquished the institution of the extended household continued to live near each other and maintained close ties, creating the new structure of "brothers' homes" (*xunei-birori*).

Even after the extended family disbanded, cooperation and mutual aid between the brothers' families continued. All the important decisions were taken communally, in the presence of the

Opposite:
Extended Jewish family, Kuba, Azerbaijan, early 20th century
Photo courtesy of Beth Hatefutsoth, The Nahum Goldmann Museum of the Jewish Diaspora, Tel Aviv

Jewish men sowing seeds
in the fields of the
Smidowitz kolkhoz,
Derbent, Dagestan, 1933
Photo courtesy of Beth
Hatefutsoth, The Nahum Goldmann
Museum of the Jewish Diaspora,
Tel Aviv

brothers, their wives, and their adult children. In most instances, part of the property remained in common ownership and was jointly administered by all the brothers' families. Such property included orchards, flour mills, ovens for drying seeds, flocks, and an oven for baking bread. Mutual economic aid played an important role in the relations between the families. Each brother would contribute from his work or his wares to his brothers' families: a tailor would make clothes for all his relatives for free, another brother would provide wood and coal for heating, and so on. On holidays the extended family gathered in the home of the eldest brother. The articles needed for the holiday were purchased jointly, and the meals were prepared together. The seating of the family members at the holiday meal followed a hierarchical order.

In recent times, the institution of the nuclear family has been strengthened, and although the phenomenon of brothers' homes has not entirely disappeared, it is no longer as common as it was in the past.

Dwellings

Caucasian Jews lived in separate quarters, and built homes adjoining one another for protection
and for the extension of mutual aid in everyday life. Secret underground passages, known only to a
select group of adults in each family, were built between the adjacent houses in order to enable the
clandestine flight of all the inhabitants of the quarter during pogroms.

The houses were built of straw and clay. As the family's economic situation improved, the
number of rooms in the house increased, and additional structures were sometimes attached
to the family compound. The houses of the wealthy were two or three stories high, and
were built of burnt bricks. The ground floor housed a shop and storerooms, and the upper
stories contained five to ten rooms. A veranda extended across the entire width of the facade,
and separate balconies were built in the back. The courtyard, which was enclosed in a brick
wall, contained stables for the horses, a granary, and an oven for baking bread. More modest

Vineyard workers in a
Jewish kolkhoz named after
Stalin, Derbent, Dagestan,
early 1940s
Photo courtesy of Beth
Hatefutsoth, The Nahum Goldmann
Museum of the Jewish Diaspora,
Tel Aviv

Drawing water, Kuba,
Azerbaijan, 1910
Photo courtesy of Haim
Agarunov, Hadera

Opposite, clockwise from
top left:

Jewish woman making
mattresses, Baku,
Azerbaijan, 2000

Preparing *duchap* (a fruit
condiment) for the winter,
Oguz, Azerbaijan, 1999

Baking bread in the
storeroom. The oven is
made of earth and is
glazed on the inside, Oguz,
Azerbaijan, 1999

Baking bread in the
kitchen, Kuba, Azerbaijan,
2001

houses had a small service yard (*eivan*) instead of a courtyard. It was not customary to plant greenery near the home.

Most houses contained two rooms, one of which was reserved exclusively for guests. The importance of hospitality (*ginog*) was so great that not even the poor could forego the possibility of housing guests in a separate room. Houses usually did not have their own kitchen. In the summer months, the vestibule, which contained an oven, functioned as a kitchen, and in the winter, food was cooked in an oven that stood in the corner of the room. On Sabbaths, use was made of an oven that was built in an alcove in a wall of the house, in which the heat was preserved during the whole day. Each house had a storeroom that contained supplies for the winter.

The inhabitants of the house ate and slept on the floor. Each morning the bedding was placed in large chests that stood within alcoves and in which most of the household objects were stored: sheets, festive clothing, jewelry, and the like. Shelves were affixed to the walls for the display of fine copper utensils. Even the most impoverished houses possessed a mirror. The floor, in most instances rammed earth, was covered by rugs that the mistress of the house had woven. The houses were lit with pottery lamps (*chiraq*) filled with crude oil. Every week, in preparation for the Sabbath, the floor and the bottom part of the walls were painted with mud (*gilov*), which was brought from small lakes in the area.

The interior of the house attested to the economic standing of its owner: the homes of the wealthy were distinguished from those of the poor by the number of rugs and the beauty of the vessels on the

shelves. Only the houses of the affluent boasted furnished guest rooms, replete with copper and silver vessels and covered with precious rugs.

Occupations

Until the October Revolution of 1917, the Jews of the Caucasus were primarily farmers, peddlers, and artisans. Some communities engaged in characteristic occupations. The Jews of Kuba and Vartashen (in the region of Azerbaijan) specialized in the rug trade and in the growing of tobacco and rice. Cultivating these crops required a vast amount of water, and the fact that water was abundant in these regions made them particularly suitable for agriculture. The water was channeled to the settlement's plantation and directed in turn to the various fields and orchards. Each farmer was required to dam the flow of water to his crops and to close the dam when it was not his turn to receive water; farmers who did not cooperate were fined. The water was allocated for free five days a week, according to a schedule prepared by the leaders of the community, and a public auction was held on Fridays for farmers who had missed their turn. They were willing to pay very high sums, as waiting for their next turn could endanger their crops.

The Jews of Vartashen also raised silkworms. Wealthy landowning families raised wheat, and frequently employed poorer Jews as laborers. Many Jews in Dagestan cultivated grapes. Every

Kerosene lamp, Ismailli,
Azerbaijan, 20th century
Copper and glass
H 41
Lent by Shamil Yakobov, Acre

vineyard owner prepared wine for home consumption, but only those with large vineyards owned industrial wineries. Winery owners often also operated factories for the production of alcohol. Every vineyard was encompassed by orchards of fruit trees, including mulberries, figs, *eibe* (a tangy local fruit), and nuts. A typical crop grown in the valleys of Dagestan was the madder, from whose roots compounds were produced (alizarin and porphyrin) which were used to dye the fibers in rugs. Three years after the planting of the madder, part of its roots could be extracted, with the plant continuing to grow for another fifteen to twenty years. The cultivation of madder provided a steady livelihood

Oil and kerosene lamps
Clay and copper,
20th century

Bowl for kneading dough,
Dagestan, 20th century
Copper

Israel Museum Collection,
purchased with the help of
Bruce Kovner, New York

and did not require a great deal of labor. Large quantities of madder roots were sold in the markets of Astrakhan, Nizhni Novgorod, and Moscow until the 1870s, when industrial dyes from France began to be imported. The loss of income from the cultivation of this plant, coupled with the heavy taxes that had to be paid for the maintenance of the local rulers' troops, left many families in serious financial straits.

Following the Civil War of 1917–21, thousands of Jews returned home after having participated in the fighting to discover that their property had been ruined or had been seized by their neighbors in their absence. Some succeeded in recovering their possessions, while others were compelled to leave their villages and migrate to the cities. Some Jews received land as part of the redistribution of lands initiated by the Communist Party. In the 1920s all-Jewish kolkhozes (collective villages) were established. In 1930, twenty-two kolkhozes, comprising 529 Jewish families, were registered in Dagestan. Interestingly, the Jewish practice of *leket* (gleanings – see Leviticus 19:9) was instituted in these kolkhozes: not all of the sheaves left after the harvest were collected, so that they could be gathered by the needy. Caucasian Jews called this custom "the gathering of clusters" (*xushe vechire*). Kolkhozes that engaged in fishing were also founded during this period. In contrast with Dagestan, which was inundated by a wave of collectivization, only a single Jewish agricultural cooperative was founded in Azerbaijan.

The postrevolutionary period was characterized by the migration of Jews to the cities, where they worked in industry and small-scale retail trade, occupations they had hardly dealt with in the past. After the Second World War, the number of Caucasian Jews in the liberal professions increased greatly.

Preparations for the Winter

The agricultural lifestyle of the peoples of the Caucasus and the harsh winters forced them to prepare ahead of time for this season. The preparations extended over the course of months, during which people came to the aid of their friends and supported orphans and widows, the sick, and needy families. The main preparations consisted in the preservation of meat, fruits, vegetables, and wine. Several related families participated in the process of preparing the meat (*sugum*), slaughtering the cows and sheep. The ritual slaughtering was performed by the local rabbi who went from house to house, with knowledgeable volunteers helping him in the work of *nikur* (the removal of the parts of the animal that are forbidden by Jewish law). The meat was cut by the young men and then transferred to the women, who washed, dried, and salted it, draining the blood out ot it to make it kosher, and then prepared sausages and other products from it. A portion of the meat was set aside for relatives and

Water jug, Dagestan,
20th century
Copper, repoussé
H 67; D 30
Lent by Yafah Hilleli,
Kiryat Bialik

needy families. During the entire period in which the meat was prepared, the rabbi, accompanied by the men who assisted him in the labor of slaughtering, would go from one family to another, making sure that the preparations were in keeping with the laws of kashrut. The process of slaughtering the cattle lasted about a month, and during this period the entire community enjoyed fresh meat.

Walnut butter was also prepared in the autumn. The shelled walnuts were ground into a paste, which was poured in shallow containers. The containers were warmed next to the stove, and when the paste turned a reddish color, it was squeezed to extract the butter from it. The remains were added to a pastry dish or eaten as a meat substitute.

The members of the community also cooperated in picking the fruit and harvesting the wheat, as well as during the calving. For about a week after a cow gives birth, it produces quantities of milk that exceed the needs of the family. Every woman who owned a cow would share the surplus milk with

Water and milk jars,
Azerbaijan, 20th century
Zinc-plated copper
H 19–30
Israel Museum Collection
Lent by Shamil Yakobov, Acre

Water jars, plates, and
vessels for warming up
food, 20th century
Clay
H 18.5–31

other women, and together they would make cheese and butter (*rughan-shiri*). To prepare the butter, sour milk (*getüg*) and water were poured into special jugs (*nire*) and churned. A tube inserted in the jug allowed the women to ascertain when the mixture had turned into butter. Garlic and chopped vegetables were added to the liquid remaining after the separation of the butter, and the resulting concoction was drunk cold. After every calving, the first milk was cooked with eggs, and the owner of the cow distributed the dish (*xurshovo*) among her relatives – a custom that persisted until the 1960s. It was customary for the relatives to return the vessels filled with water – a charm for increased milk productivity.

Vessel for measuring rice
and flour, Dagestan,
19th century
Wood
H 25; D 21
Israel Museum Collection,
purchased with the help of
Bruce Kovner, New York

Dress and Jewelry
Anatoly Binyaminov

Although some countries, including Persia (the land from which many of the Caucasian Jews originated), made a distinctive form of attire obligatory for Jews, there is little to differentiate Jewish from non-Jewish dress in the Caucasus. Jews and non-Jews used the same fabrics to make clothing and the same materials and techniques to fashion jewelry.

Women's Clothing

Women wore a petticoat or underdress (*zir-shey*) made of cotton and designed to flare at the bottom. It covered the whole body, down to the feet, and had a slit in the front with no collar; the sleeves were long and wide with no cuffs. An overdress (*bulshei* or *burshei*) worn above it was made of silk and diversely colored fabrics; it was pulled in at the waist and pleated from the waist down.

Above the overdress Jewish women habitually wore a type of robe known as *gobo* (see illustration and pattern on pp. 138–39). Usually made of cotton, the *gobo* was tight at the waist and the bottom part was long and wide like a skirt. Each sleeve had a slit from the elbow downward; the edges were decorated with silver beads and gold ribbons. For ceremonial occasions women made a silk *gobo* and for the winter, one lined with cotton or wool. Around the waist they wore leather or cloth belts with silver buckles. The cotton apron (*pishosine*) worn over the *gobo* served chiefly to hide a woman's pregnancy.

Under the petticoat women wore wide trousers (see ill. on p. 139), gathered by a threaded lace cord. The trousers were made of cotton or silk fabric, and of wool in the winter. Their edges could be seen under the petticoat and, like the *gobo*, they were decorated with silver beads and gold ribbons.

On their feet women wore soft leather shoes without hard soles (*chuvok*), brightly colored for festive occasions and black for days of mourning. Rubber galoshes (*kalushi* in Russian) were worn in winter. Instead of shoes, some women wore knitted socks with leather soles.

Around the head women tied three kinds of scarves. They covered their hair with a small square kerchief made of thin fabric (*mendil*). Over it they placed a silk or cotton scarf, or a woolen one in the winter, which was folded diagonally on the head, with the right-hand corner thrown over the back across the left shoulder. An additional scarf (also called *mendil*) was wound around the head on top of the other two. In some parts of Dagestan, the top scarf was replaced by another head covering – a kind of pouch with slits along it (*chutqu*) that reached down to the lower back. The pouch was tightly fastened with a ribbon that went from the forehead to the nape of the neck (see ill. on p. 147).

Jewish women wore their own special type of jewelry, including oval earrings of gold filigree (*gushvoy poi*) with tiny pendants dangling from them, necklaces of round gold beads, and gold chains (*zindgil-bebei*).

Opposite:
Women's silk kerchiefs and scarves, 20th century
Israel Museum Collection
Lent by the Haifa Museum of Ethnology
Lent by Avraham Avrahamov, Tel Aviv

Jewish family in traditional
dress, Buinaksk, Dagestan,
early 20th century
Photo courtesy of Avraham
Avrahamov, Tel Aviv

Left: Costume of a Muslim
Lezgian woman
(reconstruction from the
Makhachkala Museum),
Dagestan, 20th century

Right: Costume of a Muslim
Tabasaran woman
(reconstruction from the
Makhachkala Museum),
Dagestan, 20th century

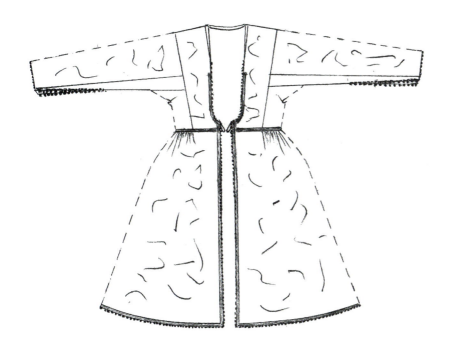

Opposite:
Woman's dress (*bulshei*)
and robe (*gobo*),
20th century
Silk, cotton, and silver
beads
Lent by the Haifa Museum of
Ethnoloy

This page:
Left: Pattern for a woman's
robe
Drawing by Miryam Adler

Below: Woman's trousers,
Kuba, Azerbaijan, 20th
century Wool and silver
beads
Israel Museum Collection,
gift of Milko Davidov, Kuba

The Jewish bride wore the whole range of clothing described above. Her petticoat was white, but her overdress, robe, and top scarf were sewn from pink-colored silk. It was customary to deck the bride with a mass of heavy gold jewelry borrowed from relatives and friends.

Men's Clothing

A man's undershirt was similar in shape to a woman's petticoat, but it had a slit on the right and ended just above the knee. Over it men wore another shirt with an upturned collar and a slit down the middle.

Above the upper shirt men also wore a *gobo* or a *cherkeska* – a dark-colored woolen coat whose lower part flared and was wrapped like a cloak. The sleeves widened above the hands. Around the waist men wore a belt of cloth, leather, or metal (or simply a piece of rope), from which they hung a dagger in its scabbard. Over the belt the *gobo* was fastened with eight or ten buttons. Together with inside pockets, it had outer pockets on either side of the chest, with nine to eleven compartments for storing rifle bullets. In winter men donned a woolen *gobo* padded with cotton.

Until the 1940s men still wore special trousers made without side seams, wide at the top and tapering downward, which were secured with a laced woolen belt.

Women's jackets, worn on festive occasions instead of the *gobo*, 20th century
Velvet, cotton, and gold-thread embroidery
Lent by the Haifa Museum of Ethnology

Most Jewish men wore fur or felt hats. Unlike other peoples in the region, the Jews wore short, round, or square-shaped hats rather than tall, conical ones. At home they tended to wear skullcaps, usually made of silk.

Until the 1940s men chiefly wore thick leather boots laced up to the knee. Leather shoes, though less common, were also worn, as were shoes with the uppers made of woven or knitted wool and shoes with felt uppers.

Children's clothes resembled those of adults in their design, but were normally produced from more colorful fabrics.

Although Western styles were already infiltrating Caucasia during World War II, it is still possible today to meet Jewish adults of Caucasian origin, including communal rabbis, who wear traditional dress.

Top left: Jewish woman
wearing basket-shaped
gold earrings, Kuba,
Azerbaijan, 2001

Top right: Traditional
basket-shaped earrings,
Derbent, Dagestan, 20th
century Gold filigree
Israel Museum Collection,
gift of Azariah Isakov, Ashkelon

Right: Modern gold
earrings, Baku, Azerbaijan,
20th century
Lent by Gila Rubinov-Ya'akov,
Holon

Opposite:
Gold necklaces and
an amuletic pendant in
the form of the Tablets of
the Law, also incised with
the Divine Name *Shaddai*,
Kuba, Azerbaijan,
20th century
Israel Museum Collection,
purchased with the help of
Bruce Kovner, New York
Lent by Liya Mikdash-
Shamailov, Jerusalem

Top: Woman's belt buckle
engraved with a Hebrew
inscription mentioning
the name of the person
who ordered or received
the belt, 1913
(See detail, p. 149)
Silver with niello, leather,
and Russian coins
L 11.5; W 8.5
Lent by the Haifa Museum of
Ethnology

Bottom: Woman's belt,
20th century
Silver with niello, leather,
and Russian coins
Lent by the Gross family,
Tel Aviv

Top: Woman's belt buckle,
20th century
Silver with niello
Lent by Rivka Gonen, Jerusalem

Bottom: Woman's belt
buckle,
20th century
Gilt-silver filigree
Israel Museum Collection,
gift of the British Friends of
the Art Museums of Israel in
honor of the 70th birthday of
Pierre Gildesgame

Top: Men's belts,
20th century
Silver with niello
and leather
The name of the owner of
the upper belt is engraved
on its buckle
Lent by the Gross family,
Tel Aviv
Lent by the Haifa Museum of
Ethnology

Bottom: Man's belt, sword,
and containers for
gunpowder, Derbent,
Dagestan, 20th century
Silver with niello, leather,
and wood
Israel Museum Collection

Opposite:
Left: Jewish woman with a
head covering (*chutqu*)
typically worn by the Avar
people in Dagestan
(reconstruction)
Silk, cotton, metal thread,
and silver beads
Israel Museum Collection,
purchased with the help of
Bruce Kovner, New York
Lent by the Haifa Museum of
Ethnology

Right: Typical man's
costume (reconstructed)
Fur, wool, and synthetic
material
Israel Museum Collection
Lent by the Haifa Museum of
Ethnology

Jewish children in
traditional dress, Baku,
Azerbaijan, 1910
Photo courtesy of Rabbi Eliezer
Mizrahi, Carmiel

Inscription engraved on a
woman's belt buckle
(detail; see p. 144)
Lent by the Haifa Museum of
Ethnology

Jewish Motifs in Caucasian Rugs

Tyilo Khizghilov

Since ancient times, rug weaving has been one of the most notable and highly developed handicrafts of the peoples and tribes of the Caucasus. The Greek historian Herodotus (ca. 480–426 BCE) wrote the following observation:

> Along the west . . . stretches the chain of the Caucasus . . . inhabited by many different tribes, most of which live off wild fruits. It is also said that there are trees here of which the leaves when crushed and mixed with water produce a dye with which the natives paint figures on their clothes, and the dye is so permanent that the designs never wash out but last as long as the material does, as if they had been woven into it when it was first made . . .[1]

During the Middle Ages, Derbent was a major center of the weaving industry. It was renowned throughout the East for its linen cloth, and accounts prior to the thirteenth century refer to the vicinity of Derbent (Bab al-Awab in Arabic) as a trading center for knotted and flat-woven rugs, especially of the *palas* type.

The peoples of Dagestan have various names for *palas* rugs: the Avars call them *dag'in*, the Qumiqs use the term *dum*, Azerbaijanis and others call them *zilu*. In another type of *palas* rug, known as *varni* or *jijim*, the tapestry and *sumaq* techniques are combined. Using the tapestry technique, the pattern is made with discountinuous weft threads; using the *sumaq* technique, the weft is wrapped manually around pairs of warp threads to form a kind of chain. The knotted and *sumaq* rugs of southern Dagestan and northern Azerbaijan are as sought after today as they were in the past.

Objects dating from the tenth century, unearthed during archaeological excavations in the region, provide further evidence that the weaving of rugs was already a developed art there in ancient times. These finds include items connected with weaving, such as special bone implements used to tighten the knots on the rug. Until the mid-thirteenth century, high-quality linen for the weaving industry and madder (*marena*) and saffron plants for the manufacture of dyes were exported from Caucasia to the East. Popular crafts of the region – processing linen, wool, and silk or weaving fabrics and rugs – helped to supply most of the local population's own requirements. Individual regions excelled in certain crafts and have since maintained their reputation for high-quality products. Local techniques were passed on from generation to generation, and the handiwork of local craftsmen has always been in great demand.

Rug making was a female occupation, and some women gained renown as first-rate artisans. Most of them usually spun their own wool as their families owned flocks of sheep. The madder plant, from which a red dye was extracted, and the saffron plant, used for a yellow dye, were both cultivated by Jews. The indigo plant, which yielded a blue dye, was imported to the Caucasus by Jewish merchants. The Mountain Jews supplied markets with these goods until the mid-nineteenth century, when they were forced to halt their operations because of the nomadic way of life imposed

Opposite:
A rug weaver
(reconstruction from the
Museum of Ethnography,
Derbent, Dagestan)

on them by Muslim intolerance. However, after the Soviet regime established workers' collectives and home industries in the 1930s, Caucasian Jewish women resumed the art of weaving. They continue to produce high-quality woven goods, chiefly in Kuba but also in Derbent.

Although the techniques, colors, and normal composition of Jewish rug weaving fall within the sphere of Caucasian art in general, one group of patterns from the nineteenth century – *ju'ud-cheshne* (Jewish design), as it is called by the Lezgian and Tabasaran populations – evidently relates to a characteristically Jewish artistic idiom. The same "Jewish designs" appear, however, in the rugs made by other peoples of Dagestan. One explanation for the ubiquity of these designs is the presence of a large Jewish population in that area long before Arab settlers arrived. From 737, Jews and other ethnic groups in the Caucasus started to undergo a process of Islamization which continued, with varying degrees of success, until the region was annexed by Russia. Many peoples of Dagestan, including the Lezgians, Tabasarans, and Tatars, believe that their ancestors were Jews, and tell stories and legends about their Jewish roots.

For generations past, the study of Kabbalah has formed part of the tradition of the Mountain Jews. Libraries owned by rabbis and other private individuals still contain works on Jewish mysticism and "practical" Kabbalah such as *The Book of Raziel, Sefer Yetzirah*, teachings of the Ari (Rabbi Isaac Luria), the Zohar (or Book of Splendor), and *Sefer ha-Yashar*. Chapters from the Song of Songs, extracts from the Zohar, and mystical poems are read in synagogue on Friday night, prior to the Sabbath eve services. Magic also played a role in the daily life of Caucasian Jews – in wedding ceremonies and funerals, in treating various ailments, using spells, invoking rain, welcoming the spring, and marking the termination of the Sabbath after *havdalah*. In Jewish art forms, particularly rug weaving, one may also find motifs to which magical powers were ascribed and which were handed down by the weavers from one generation to the next.

"Jewish design" rugs may be divided into two categories: *sha'am-dor* or *sha'am-agaji* "candle tree" rugs (*sha'am* means "candle" and *agaji* "tree" in Turkish; *dor* means "tree" in Persian), which display the motif of a candle tree (actually a fir), sometimes resembling a menorah; and *ezhdaha mar* "dragon snake" rugs. Those belonging to the first category are usually small. Against a terra-cotta background (see illustration on p. 153, left), six large forms face each other symmetrically; four of them resemble trees with triangular tops and with trunks ending in a triangular base. They appear as two pairs on opposite sides of the rug. Two rhomboids are located in the middle, each containing nineteen small red and white rhomboids. Between the large forms, in the central portion of the rug, eight pairs of long-tailed birds are arranged symmetrically. The candle tree and bird motifs reappear in traditional songs of the Mountain Jews associated with the welcoming of spring. [2]

Another example of the *sha'am-dor* group (see ill. on p. 153, right) displays rows of candle trees in a checkered pattern. The background is dark blue with red, white, and beige motifs. A *sumaq* rug of the type known as *sumaqche* ("small *sumaq*"; see ill. on p. 157) has four pairs of candle trees dividing a series of five rhomboids. In another rug (see ill. on p. 156), two rows of candle trees flank square medallions. The menorah-like pattern in another *sumaq* rug (see ill. on p. 154, top) may perhaps have evolved from the candle-tree motif.

The dragon and snake (*ezhdaha mar*) figures in the second group of "Jewish design" rugs have been well-known symbols in the Far East ever since ancient times.[3] In the Talmud and Jewish mysticism they are considered to be protectors: "Rabbi Shim'on ben Menasya said: 'Woe for the loss of a great servant! Had not the serpent been cursed, every Israelite would have had two serpents at his disposal – one to be sent north and the other south, to bring him costly gems, precious stones, and pearls'" (Sanhedrin 59b). According to *Sefer Yetzirah* (6.2), Tali the dragon rules over the universe (physical and heavenly bodies) "like a king on his throne." The dragon is also held to be the thirteenth sign of the zodiac, positioned above the other twelve signs. [4]

The "dragon rug" (see ill. on p. 155) was presumably a kind of amulet protecting the home. This type of rug was hard to find, made by the weavers for their own use and not for sale. As a secondary decorative element, the dragon motif also appears on rugs produced in southern Dagestan, mainly by the Lezgians, who also view it as a protective charm.

The "Jewish design" rugs surveyed above were woven up to the nineteenth century in a few villages of southern Dagestan. They were discovered in the course of field work in that area during the years 1980–90. Not having been designed for commercial purposes, these rugs were scarce and little publicity was given to them. Attempts are now being made to copy them, but only few of the original motifs are employed, and the resulting ornamentation is therefore sparse and plain.

---

1 Herodotus, *The Histories*, trans. Aubrey de Sélincourt, rev. A. R. Burn (Penguin Classics, 1972), p. 123.

2 On ceremonies held to welcome the spring, see in the chapter on the cycle of the year, p. 86.

3 Regarding the place occupied by these figures in the life of Caucasian Jews, see in the chapter on beliefs and ceremonies, p. 118.

4 See the Zohar, Pinhas. Jewish familiarity with the literature of "practical" Kabbalah on the one hand and with the Muslim dragon motif on the other leads me to conjecture that the form on the rug (p. 155) might be viewed as a dragon incorporating the mystical Tree of Ten *Sefirot* (Divine Emanations), with the Hebrew letter *shin* on either side of its head, associating it with the name *Shaddai*.

Candle-tree motif in
knotted rugs, Dagestan,
19th century
Left: From the village of
Gimadi
Right: From the village of
Ahti
(Drawings by Anna Tsafin)

Top: Menorah motif in a *sumaq* rug from the village of Ikra, Dagestan, 19th century

Bottom: Dragon motif in a knotted rug from the village of Ahti, Dagestan, 19th century

(Drawings made and lent by Tyilo Khizghilov)

Sumaq rug with dragon
motif from the village of
Ahti, Dagestan,
19th century
Wool, L 260; W 160
Lent by Tyilo Khizghilov,
Jerusalem

Opposite:
Sumaq rug from the
Samur region, Dagestan,
19th century
Wool, L 300; W 200

This page:
Sumaq rug (*sumaqche*)
from Derbent, Dagestan,
19th century
Wool, L 200; W 110

Lent by Tyilo Khizghilov,
Jerusalem

Bibliography

Agarunov, S. "Mountain Jews." *Tribuna* (Moscow) 10 (1928). Russian

Agarunov, Y. and M. Agarunov. *Tatic-Russian Dictionary*. Moscow, 1997. Russian

Al-Istakhri, A. "The Roads and the Kingdoms." *Collection of Place and Tribe Descriptions in the Caucasus* (Tiflis, 1901). Trans. by N. Karaulov. Russian

Altshuler, *Jews of the Eastern Caucasus* Altshuler, M. *Jews of the Eastern Caucasus*. Jerusalem, 1990. Hebrew

Altshuler, M., Pinhasy, Y., and Zand, M. *Bukharan Jews and Mountain Jews: Two Communities in the Southern Soviet Union*. Jerusalem, 1973. Hebrew

Anisimov, "Mountain Jews" Anisimov, I. "Mountain Jews of the Caucasus." *Collection of Ethnographic Articles* (Dashkov Museum of Ethnography) 3 (1888). Russian

Arbel and Magal, *In the Land of the Golden Fleece* Arbel, R. and Magal, L. (eds.). *In the Land of the Golden Fleece: A History of the Jews of Georgia and Their Culture*. Exh. cat., Beth Hatefutsoth, The Nahum Goldmann Museum of the Jewish Diaspora. Tel Aviv, 1992. Hebrew

Avishai, "The Mountain Jews" Avishai, M. "The Mountain Jews – Between Past and Present." In *The Jews of the Soviet Union,* edited by D. Prital, 154–63. Hebrew

Azerbaijan Carpet. Baku, 1985

Babalikashvili, "Jewish Inscriptions" N. Babalikashvili. "Jewish Inscriptions on Tombstones in the Caucasus." *Semitic Studies* (Tbilisi, 1983). Russian

Bezhanov, "Vartashen" Bezhanov, M. "Jews of the Vartashen Village." *Collection of Place and Tribe Descriptions in the Caucasus* (Tiflis, 1900). Russian

Bolshon, M. "New Agricultural Workers." *Tribune* (Moscow) 1–2 (1928). Russian

Chirkov, *Daghestan Decorative Art* Chirkov, D. *Daghestan Decorative Art*. Moscow, 1971

Chorny, *Book of Travels* Chorny, J. *Book of Travels in the Caucasus*. St. Petersburg, 1884. Hebrew

Chorny, "Jews in the Land of the Caucasus" —— . "Jews in the Lands of the Caucasus." *Hamaggid* 14–18, 38 (1868). Hebrew

Chorny, *Jews of the Caucasus* —— . *Jews of the Caucasus*. Tiflis, 1869. Russian

Collection (Tiflis) *Collection of Place and Tribe Descriptions in the Caucasus* (Tiflis) (1870). 3d ed. Russian

Collection of Place and Tribe Descriptions in the Caucasus (Tiflis) (1884). 4th ed. Russian

David, Y. *A History of the Jews in the Caucasus*. Tel Aviv, 1989. Russian

Ethnographic Survey on the Bride Price and Dowry of Caucasian Jews. 3d ed. Moscow, 1890. Russian

Gadjiev, G. *Pre-Islamic Religions and Customs of the Peoples of Dagestan*. Moscow, 1991. Russian

Goldelman, M. "Jews in the Ethnic History of the Khazars." *Newsletter of the Hebrew University of Moscow* 8 (1995). Russian

Grafman, *Crowning Glory* Grafman, R. *Crowning Glory: Silver Torah Ornament of The Jewish Museum, New York*. New York, 1996

Grafman, *50 Rimmonim* —— . *50 Rimmonim: a Selection of Torah Finials from a European Family Collection*. Exh. cat., The Cymbalista Synagogue and Jewish Heritage Center, The Judaica Museum, Tel-Aviv University. Tel Aviv, 1998. Hebrew

Hanegbi and Yaniv, *Afghanistan* Hanegbi, Z. and Yaniv, B. *Afghanistan: the Synagogue and the Jewish Home*. The Center for Jewish Art, The Hebrew University of Jerusalem. Jerusalem, 1981. Hebrew

Harkabi, A. and Katznelson, Y. L. (eds.). *Jewish Encyclopedia*. Vols. 9 and 14. St. Petersburg, 1908–13. Russian

Ikhi'ilov, M. "Caucasian Jews." *The Peoples of Dagestan* (Moscow, 1955). Russian

"The Jews of the Caucasus." *The Platform for Soviet Jewish Communities* 4–7 (1927). Russian

—— . "Large Families and Patriarchy among the Jews of the Caucasus." *Soviet Ethnography* (1950). Russian

Kasdai, *The Kingdom of Ararat*   **Kasdai, Z.** *The Kingdom of Ararat.* Odessa, 1912. Hebrew

Kasdai, "Travel Letters"   —— . "Travel Letters." *Hatzefirah* (1893): 113. Hebrew

Kobichev, V. *Living Quarters of the Peoples of North Caucasus in the 19th and 20th Centuries.* Moscow, 1982. Russian

—— . "Living Quarters of the Peoples of the Northern Caucasus in the 19th Century." *Soviet Ethnography* 3 (1957). Russian

Kozubsky, Y. "Description of Handicrafts in the Dagestan Province." *Publications of the First Convention on Handicrafts in the Caucasus.* Tiflis, 1902. Russian

Kudriavtzev, A. *Great City on the Caspian Sea.* Makhachkala, 1982. Russian

Kurdov, K. "Mountain Jews in the Shemakhin Region in Baku Province." *Russian Journal of Anthropology* (1912). Russian

Lavrov, L. *The Ethnography of the Caucasus.* Leningrad, 1982. Russian

Levy, G. "Everyday Life and Customs of the Caucasian Jews of Kuba." *Voskhod* (1901). Russian

Maggid, D. "Jews in the Caucasus." In *Jews in the Southern Reaches of Russia.* Vol. 1. Petrograd, 1917. Russian

Manoakh, B. *Shalmaneser's Captives.* Jerusalem, 1984. Russian

Miller, *Tats*   **Miller, B.** *Tats – Their Geographical Dispersion and Their Dialects.* Baku, 1929. Russian

Morzakhanov, Y. *Outline of the History of Ethnographic Research on the Jews of the Caucasus.* Moscow, 1994. Russian

—— . *The Contemporary Jewish Family in Kabardino-Balkaria.* Moscow, 1994. Russian

—— . *The Jews of the Caucasus: An Annotated Bibliographical Guide.* Moscow, 1994. Russian

Nemirovich-Danchenko, V. *Militant Israel.* St. Petersburg, 1880. Russian

Razina, Cherkasova, and Kantsedikas, *Folk Art*   **Razina, T., Cherkasova, N.,** and **Kantsedikas, A.** *Folk Art in the Soviet Union.* Leningrad, 1989

"Rural Living Quarters of the People of the Caucasus in the 19th Century." In *Ethnographic Writings on the Caucasus.* Moscow-Leningrad, 1962. Russian

Shikhsaidov, A. *Dagestan in the 10th to 14th Centuries.* Makhachkala, 1975. Russian

"The Geographical-Economic Region of Kuba-Khachmaz, Soviet Azerbaijan." Bulletin of the Geographical Institute of the Academy of Azerbaijan (1958). Russian

Shrire, *Hebrew Amulets*   **Shrire, T.** *Hebrew Amulets.* London, 1966

Tuyakbayeva, *Epigraphic Decorations*   **Tuyakbayeva, B. T.** *Epigraphic Decorations in Architectural Complexes According to Ahmed Yasawi.* Alma Ata, 1989. Russian

Weissenberg, S. "The Mountain Jews". Jewish Antiquities (St. Petersburg) 6 (1913). Russian

Yaniv, "Content and Form"   **Yaniv, B.** "Content and Form in the Flat Torah Finials from Eastern Iran and Afghanistan." *Pe'amim* 79 (1999): 96–128. Hebrew

Yishai, "The Jewish Settlement"   **Yishai, A.** and **N.** "The Jewish Settlement in the Eastern Caucasus." *Pe'amim* 81 (2000): 94–95. Hebrew

Additional Donors to the Collection

Zichriya Altbauer, Jerusalem

Ludmilla Izmailov, Modi'in

Yaffa Khaimov, Yeruham

The Makhachkala synagogue, Dagestan

Esther Mikdash, Kuba, Azerbaijan

Yaffa Mikdash, Kuba, Azerbaijan

Esther Rakhanayev, Kiryat Bialik

Clara Uriayev, Kuba, Azerbaijan

Photographic Credits

© The Israel Museum, Jerusalem, by:
Avshalom Avital: pp. 54, 80, 81, 112–15, 128–34,
138–47, 155–57

Peter Lanyi: pp. 17, 22, 36, 41, 43 (bottom), 44, 45, 61, 93–95,
98, 99, 101, 105, 110, 116

Liya Mikdash-Shamailov: pp. 50, 58, 69, 84, 87, 103, 107, 127
(top and bottom right), 137, 150

Faig Gonagov, Kuba, Azerbaijan: pp. 82, 83, 85, 108, 109, 115
(far right), 119

Gamlet Gasanov, Baku, Azerbaijan: pp. 88

Mikhail Kirilov, Makhachkala, Dagestan: p. 16

© The Center for Jewish Art, The Hebrew University
of Jerusalem, by:
Boris Khaimovich: pp. 6, 14, 64, 66–68, 70, 72, 74, 76, 77

Michael Kheifets: pp. 24, 71

© Rivka Gonen: pp. 75, 127 (bottom left), 142 (top left)